Leadership Lessons from My Fathers

Essential Wisdom for Leadership and Life

By
Ken Hartley

HARTLEY LEADERSHIP

Copyright ©2022 by Ken Hartley

For permission requests, speaking inquiries, training inquiries, and bulk order purchase options, you may contact the authors directly at:
ken@hartleyleadership.com

All rights reserved. No part of this book may be reproduced by any mechanical, photographic, or electronic process, or in the form of a phonographic recording; nor may it be stored in a retrieval system, transmitted, or otherwise copied for public or private use—other than for "fair use" as brief quotations embodied in articles and reviews—without prior written permission of the publisher.

Published by Transformational Truths Global, LLC
www.hartleyleadership.com

Scriptures marked NKJV are taken from the NEW KING JAMES VERSION (NKJV): Scripture taken from the NEW KING JAMES VERSION®. Copyright © 1982 by Thomas Nelson, Inc. Used by permission. All rights reserved.
Scriptures marked KJV are taken from the KING JAMES VERSION (KJV): KING JAMES VERSION, public domain.
Scriptures marked NLT are taken from the HOLY BIBLE, NEW LIVING TRANSLATION (NLT): Scriptures taken from the HOLY BIBLE, NEW LIVING TRANSLATION, Copyright © 1996, 2004, 2007 by Tyndale House Foundation. Used by permission of Tyndale House Publishers, Inc., Carol Stream, Illinois 60188. All rights reserved. Used by permission.

This publication is designed to provide accurate and authoritative information with regard to the subject matter covered. It is sold with the understanding that the publisher and author are not engaged in rendering legal, accounting, psychological, or other professional advice. If legal advice or other expert assistance is required, the service of a competent professional should be sought. This book represents the ideas from Ken Hartley which are derived his years of leadership, ministry, biblical study, speaking, and training on leadership.

ISBN: 978-1-7333818-1-9 (Paperback)
ISBN: 978-1-7333818-2-6 (Hardcover)
ISBN: 978-1-7333818-3-3 (ePUB)
ISBN: 978-1-7333818-4-0 (Audio)

First Edition

Contents

Praise for "Leadership Lessons from My Fathers": i
Acknowledgments iii
Foreword v
Introduction vii
Prologue: June 17, 2000 1
Section I: My Earthly Father 3
  Part I: Dr. Kenneth R. Hartley, Sr. 5
    Chapter 1: Passion 7
    Chapter 2: Lying 11
    Chapter 3: Tomatoes 15
    Chapter 4: People 19
    Chapter 5: The Lawn Mower 23
    Chapter 6: A Pound and a Half of Roast 27
    Chapter 7: Expectations 31
    Chapter 8: Reader's Digest Critics 35
    Chapter 9: Mr. Fix It 39
    Chapter 10: Motivation and Inspiration 43
    Chapter 11: The Fishing Pole in the Corner 47
Section II: Spiritual Fathers 53
  Part II: Dr. James D. Whitmire 55
    Chapter 12: Hard Work and Failure 57
    Chapter 13: Childlike Wonder 61
  Part III: Rev. Fred J. Ward 67
    Chapter 14: Nothing Personal 69
    Chapter 15: Stallions and Thoroughbreds 73

    Chapter 16: Hit Dogs 77

    Chapter 17: Being a Genius 81

    Chapter 18: Bill 83

    Chapter 19: Get Your Glove, Sidney 87

    Chapter 20: Drain the Swamp 91

    Chapter 21: Count the Cost 93

    Chapter 22: The Leaf 97

    Chapter 23: Chameleons 101

    Chapter 24: Charlie's Poop 105

Part IV: Dr. Ron Phillips Sr. 109

    Chapter 25: Be Real 111

    Chapter 26: Timing 115

    Chapter 27: Believe the Best 119

    Chapter 28: Forgive Others 121

    Chapter 29: Don't Quit! 123

Part V: Governor Mike Huckabee 127

    Chapter 30: Uncommon Ground 129

    Chapter 31: The Greatest Among You 133

    Chapter 32: Find the Loners 137

Part VI: Bad Fathers 141

    Chapter 33: Bad Fathers 143

Conclusion: June 17, 2000 151

About Ken Hartley: 157

Endnotes 159

Praise for "Leadership Lessons from My Fathers":

Ken Hartley is an incredibly engaging speaker and author. I have watched his illusions drop open people's jaws and his teaching open their minds and hearts. He never ceases to amaze everyone who sees him! As a lifetime entrepreneur and owner of several highly successful businesses, I know leadership. Ken is a leader and is gifted at communicating those principles to others. Read this book and do what it says! You'll be a better leader and like Ken and me—you'll be Wired Differently!
Todd Saylor
Wired Differently

Great leaders develop great leaders! One of the greatest things that a leader can do for their followers is to create an ecosystem in which leadership can be practiced. Imagine a Leadership gym where leadership muscles can be developed! Ken's new book lays out very practical ways to do just that! You will become a more impactful leader when you read, apply and duplicate the principles in this outstanding leadership book.
-Dave Kauffman, Speaker and Author of the Bestselling book- People Centered Leadership

I love how Ken intertwines his experiences and life lessons as he shares his journey of self-discovery from his earthly and spiritual fathers. Written in a relatable and easy way to digest, this captivating and thought-provoking book provides a unique perspective on the role of a father.
Shawn Dorrough
Investment Counselor
Dallas TX

As a young college student, I was privileged to learn much from Dr. Kenneth Hartley ("Doc" to me and so many others). The wisdom he gifted me with and the leadership skills he taught have stayed with me for decades and are invaluable. And the apple doesn't fall far from the leadership tree! Ken Hartley is a gifted writer, motivating teacher, and effective leader who has greatly impacted my life. I am honored to call him my brother and dear friend. I know "Doc" would be very proud!
Michael Moore
Westwood Baptist Church
Murfreesboro, TN

Everywhere you turn, there is a lesson to be learned from life—if you know where to look. Ken does a masterful job of taking seemingly big and small life events and turning them into lessons that you can apply to your life to learn how to lead more effectively. As you read, be prepared to be strategically drawn into the stories and then to walk away with your own thoughts of how you are going to apply all the lessons into your own life.
Chris Rollins
President of Rollins Performance Group, Inc.

In the Fall of 1987, I began to watch a father and son relationship that's turned into a lifetime of friendship and ministry moments for me. Dr. Ken Hartley and his son were an incredible example of relational leadership that still blesses me today. Thank you for an example of doing it right. The stories and lessons in this book reflect relational leadership and I believe they'll help all of us in our leadership.
Jamie Parker
Worship Pastor, South Fulton Baptist Church, South Fulton, Tennessee

ACKNOWLEDGMENTS

This book would not exist without the love and support of so many people.

First of all, I want to obviously thank my father, Dr. Kenneth R. Hartley, Sr. I am the person I am today in large part because of him, and I am eternally grateful for his influence as well as his tough love. He remains as he always was: my hero.

To Dr. Jim Whitmire for being willing to look past the irritation of thousands of curious questions from a kid and for seeing something in me that I did not see in myself: thank you!

To Fred Ward. Our golden ages of ministry years we spent together in Huntingdon, Tennessee were some of the greatest of my life. When Fred left this world for heaven, a piece of my heart went with him. I'm beyond grateful that he loved me enough to tell me the truth.

To Dr. Ron Phillips. Thank you for showing me the power being authentically you. Thank you for believing in a 34-year-old kid who thought he knew something but didn't. Thank you for your enduring patience, ever present wisdom, and loving candor. I am a better person because I've known and served with you.

To Governor Mike Huckabee. "The greatest among you is the servant of all." You have modeled this every day I've been around you and each day was a lesson in both your words and deeds. You, sir, are the greatest.

To Lois Ward- I know living without Fred is the hardest thing you've ever done. You model class and one of the greatest hearts for the Lord I've ever known. Thank you for your love and encouragement and for writing the foreword to the book.

To the people at Abba's House who have loved and encouraged me in these endeavors, you have my heartfelt gratitude.

For my family, both immediate and extended, who has heard some of these stories hundreds of times and still manages to smile as if you haven't—thank you for your kind indulgence and encouragement. I pray these stories will live in the hearts of your children's children and empower them to be the leaders I know they will become. I love you all.

Despite the irony, I am lovingly dedicating this book to my mother, Glenna Hartley. This book would never have been written without her encouragement. During her last days on this earth, she listened to the chapters of this book through smiles and tears, all the while prodding me to keep going and finish it. She finished her journey on this earth before this book was finished, but her fingerprint on this project is indelible. I love you and miss you, Mom, but I know your joy is complete in the Presence of our Lord Jesus and in the presence of the man you loved for your entire life with all of your heart: My Dad.

Foreword

I have known Ken Hartley since he was fresh out of college. Alongside my late husband, Fred Ward, I also had the privilege of working in ministry with his Dad. Dr. Kenneth Hartley embodied class and leadership. We were so blessed to know him and his sweet wife, Glenna.

Having known Ken for most of his life, I have observed his growth through the years as a leader in ministry and ultimately a leader in life. He has always had natural talents and abilities, but he doesn't simply rely on those as others might do. He actively works on his growth and refuses to settle for less.

He has always had a desire to go deeper and climb higher. Fred saw something in Ken that he didn't yet see in himself, and they were both better people because they knew each other.

Some of the stories in this book brought laughter while others brought tears. In both cases, the stories and the lessons need to be told. The lessons here are too valuable to be left alone. For years, Fred talked about writing some of these stories into a book, but it didn't happen. I am grateful that Ken has taken the time to write some of Fred's stories as well as the lessons from his Dad and others who have made an impact on him.

I originally knew Ken as a gifted singer, but his speaking has come into its own and it is a pleasure to watch it unfold. To see him traveling the world and helping others in their leadership journey is extremely gratifying. I know Fred was always so proud of him and I believe he still is today.

Let the stories and lessons in this book make you a better leader and hopefully, a better person. I know they have done that for me.

Lois Ward
Huntingdon, Tennessee

INTRODUCTION

I was thrust into leadership at a very young age (eighteen), and I ended up learning a great deal by trial and *a lot* of error. I was also privileged to learn from some really good mentors. In this book, I will share what I learned from their wisdom.

I have also been a student of leadership for years, reading as many books as I could on the subject as well as earning my certification from the John Maxwell Team in leadership, speaking, and training. Since then, I have traveled internationally to speak about leadership, communication, and personal growth for the last several years. **I exist to empower leaders to lead and communicate with authenticity.** I believe that this book will help put you on that journey. If you're already on the leadership journey, I believe it will help you raise your game in several areas.

Before we jump in, I want to say a few things. The lessons I learned from my father and my spiritual fathers are applicable to every area of your life, regardless of your background. Let me say at the outset that I am a person of faith. As a believer in Jesus Christ, my faith shapes some of what you're going to read. If you're not a believer, these lessons will still be applicable to you. I just wanted to make it clear as to what my worldview is and where I'm coming from before we begin.

My leadership journey began before I was eighteen. It began when I was much younger with my father's guidance. My father was a teacher for all of his life. He taught professionally at the graduate and collegiate level, but he also found lessons to teach in everyday life. I understood some of those lessons immediately, while others came into my awareness later in life. His wit and wisdom still follow me today, and I thought they were worth passing on, so I wrote this book.

These are the lessons I am passing along to you in this book. The chapters are divided into stories (all true), leadership lessons, and applications to help you in life and on your leadership journey. My hope and prayer are that they impact you and your loved ones for years to come.

Ken Hartley
Chattanooga, Tennessee
www.hartleyleadership.com

Prologue

June 17, 2000

8:00 p.m.

There he lay—silently, shallowly breathing. I sat in a chair to the side of his hospital bed, watching carefully to make sure my feet didn't step on the seemingly endless nests of wires and tubes that were connected to him. Cancer is such a thief. I hate it. Despite never drinking or smoking a day in his life, eating well, and exercising, Dad had cancer. Life is so unfair. As I sat there, looking at the shell that contained what was left of him, my thoughts drifted back to the previous week.

I remembered how alert he was when I first arrived at the hospital. He was weak, but he still flashed his trademark smile that always lit up a room. We reminisced about some fun times we had together.

I remembered the doctor coming in and talking with us. The fake smile on his face told me he was trying to be kind, but he knew the imminent and inevitable outcome. When he was leaving, he said, "Good luck to you." In truth, he was saying, "Goodbye," and he and I both knew it.

There was a steady stream of visitors at the door that my mother was fielding. She was doing what she had done for nearly fifty years—protecting my father and doing what was best for him. Although the visitors meant well, their timing could not have been worse.

My thoughts went back to how badly his health had slipped in the last three days. For example, his inability to roll over, much less do anything else. I remembered pushing him in a wheelchair down the hospital hallway so he could look outside at the sunset. After being cooped up in that hospital room for a few days, I thought he would want to stay for a while and take in the sunset, but after about forty-five seconds, he asked me to roll him back to his room and put him back into bed.

I remembered the physical indignities he had suffered in the last twenty-four hours; and I thought about how I held him and cleaned him up, and he expressed his dismay when he said, "I can't believe this is happening to me."

I snapped back to the present moment.

Mom came back into the room. She was exhausted. Some close friends had arrived and began fielding the visitors so Mom could sit by Dad's bedside.

The next two hours passed slowly. I watched her hug and kiss him. I watched her whisper softly in his ear how much she loved him and how honored she was to have been his wife. During the afternoon, he responded, but now . . . silence.

Around 11 p.m., his breathing became shallower. Then there was more time between his breaths. The nurse came in to check his vital signs, which wasn't necessary, but she was being extremely kind and attentive.

Mom asked, "Is he comfortable?"

The nurse replied, "Oh yes. We've done absolutely everything we can to make him comfortable. He isn't suffering at all." Mom managed a weak smile back at her and thanked her. Her strength was incredible.

Around 11:45 p.m., my brother, my mother, and I stood by his bedside, arm in arm, and prayed. At 11:51 p.m., he stopped breathing.

Through my tears, I called the nurse and asked her to come to the room. She arrived at 12:06 a.m., and he was pronounced dead at 12:07 a.m.

There on the hospital bed lay the earthly remains of my hero.
My father.
He was gone.
I looked at my watch. It was 12:08 a.m. on June 18, 2000.
It was Father's Day.

Section I

My Earthly Father

PART I

DR. KENNETH R. HARTLEY, SR.

My dad was Dr. Kenneth Hartley, Sr. He was raised on farms in southwest Missouri and eastern Oklahoma. He worked hard on those farms and raised some award-winning animals. Despite his rural upbringing, he was a classically trained musician.

He became one of the first people in his family to earn a college degree. He served as a missionary to Alaska before it became a state. For many years, he directed the music at various churches, including a large church (over one thousand members in attendance) in Birmingham, Alabama. Although he led singing and worship in churches for the rest of his life, that vocation was not his passion. He was a teacher. He lived to pour into others.

It was this passion that led him to earn a master's degree from a seminary and finally a doctorate in music education from Florida State University.

Dad began teaching music students on the graduate level at New Orleans Theological Seminary but ultimately decided to return to the collegiate level because he felt the students were more pliable and open to learn. He stayed there for the rest of his life.

He was the chairman of the music department at Belmont University in Nashville, Tennessee, for a few years, and then he left to go to the same position at Union University in Jackson, Tennessee, where he stayed for thirty years. During his tenure, he impacted thousands of students. Yes, he was an incredible teacher with a commanding knowledge of music, but his greatest impact wasn't simply in music. It was in *life*.

He would take ordinary instances and turn them into unforgettable life lessons. He taught them to his family. He taught them to his students, many of whom saw him as the father they never had. I hope you'll learn as much from them as others have over the years. For you, the reader, here is the gentle and profound wisdom from my father, Dr. Kenneth Hartley, Sr.

4 Generations of Hartleys

Chapter 1

Passion

I was beyond excited. As a college student who had floundered for three semesters, having fun, hanging out with fraternity friends, occasionally showing up for classes, and squeaking by, I now had a clear direction for my life. The reason I had so little focus on my studies was due to a lack of understanding of what I wanted to do. I mean, why focus on a subject when I had no guarantee I was going to use it or gain any benefits from it?

Now I had clarity. I was going into an honorable profession—one which my father had done for part of his life. I was going into full-time ministry.

I was one of those kids who was naturally good at music. I could match pitch and sing solos by the time I was four. At five years of age, my father put me in front of a large collegiate crowd and had me sing a solo from an oratorio.

I loved acting and did many community theater productions in my elementary and teenage years. I always wanted to have a great acting role within a musical production, but every time a director heard me sing, I was relegated to a solo and the acting part went to someone else. After my auditions, the directors would say, "There are many who could do this part, but you're the only one who can carry that singing part."

As a result, I sang . . . many times through resentment. And the older I got, the more the resentment grew. In fact, once I got into middle school, I joined the band so I would no longer have to sing. I started playing the trombone and hid in the section. I was a mediocre instrumentalist at best, but somehow, being hidden felt right to me.

In my junior year in high school, after a jazz band rehearsal, that all changed when the band director heard me sing, and he said, "I had no idea you sang like that." Fast forward a month, and I was singing "You're the Inspiration" at the opening of the Miss Tennessee Pageant.

No matter how far I ran from it, singing always followed me. When I went to college, singing made sense from the standpoint of scholarships. I didn't want my family to be severely impacted financially by my college tuition, so I used the singing scholarships to pay for what I wanted.

There was a problem, though. . . . I had *no* idea what I wanted to do. I majored in psychology and sociology. I was also flying planes and seriously considering going into the military to fly in the US Navy, Air Force, or Marines. I was about to sign up for Officer Candidate School, but after a special speaker at our college inspired me, my direction changed. Suddenly, I knew what I was supposed to do: ministry.

And then I told God, "I'll do anything you want in ministry, except music." Just an FYI, if you want to know the definition of humor, try telling God what you are or are not going to do and watch what happens. I knew in my heart of hearts that music ministry was what I was going to do for this season in my life.

There was a great amount of peace in finally knowing. I could now focus on my studies. I could focus fully on music. I could take classes in theology and ministry. It was incredibly exciting.

My dad was the first one I told once I knew. I approached him with great excitement and said, "Dad! I know what I'm supposed to do now! I finally have that direction I've been looking for!"

"Great, Son, what is it?"

"I'm going to be in full-time music ministry! What do you think?"

Dad paused for a moment, then looked at me and said, "If you can do anything else . . . do it."

I sat there and looked at him with a bit of shock on my face. He patted me on the shoulder and walked away, and I sat there deflated.

I talked to him again a couple of days later and asked him why he would say something so discouraging to me. Dad smiled that wise smile and replied, "It wasn't bad. I wasn't trying to be discouraging. I just know ministry. If you can do something else, you will. If it's what you're supposed to do and what you're passionate about, then you'll do fine. . . . So, the real question is: are you sure this is what you're supposed to do and are you passionate about it? Just think about it."

I did think about it for a few more days. I went back to him and told him I was passionate about it and it was what I was called to do and be. He smiled and said, "Great, Son. Go for it."

I spent the next thirty-three years doing just that. And when I wanted to quit (which was many times) and my tank felt empty, I found the fuel to stoke the fire again. That fire was my *passion*.

Passion is what makes you get up one more time and try again. Passion is what will take you beyond your natural abilities. Passion will pour fuel into your soul when it is running on empty fumes. Passion, simply put, is what you were created for. It's why you're here.

> **"Passion, simply put, is what you were created for. It's why you're here."**

Think about what wakes you up in the morning and excites you. It's what keeps you from sleeping in the evenings because you're so excited about it!

Here's a great question to answer concerning your passion: "If I had $10 million in my bank account, what would I be doing?" Forget vacations and recreation. You could do that for a few months or even a year or so, but after a while, your soul would start longing for purpose and fulfillment. What would your heart long to do? What problem in this world do you believe you could solve? Who would you help? How would you help them? How would you add value to them? What excites you so much that you want to do it every single day? And the big question: why are you here on this earth?

All those clues are road signs pointing you to your passion. Here's the amazing part: Dad knew what my passion was before I did. In fact, he helped me find my first job within my passion *before* I had any of these conversations with him. It started as a job, and it turned into a thirty-three-year passion, full of changed lives. Your passion will change other people's lives for the better, too . . . *if* you have the courage to pursue it.

Leadership Lesson: Find your passion and do it!

APPLICATION:

- Think about what you would be doing if money wasn't an issue.

-

-

- What wakes you up every morning with anticipation and excitement about your day?

-

-

- What skills and/or talents do you have?

-

-

- What problem do you see in the world that you believe you could solve?

-

-

- It's been said that at the intersection of our passion and skills lies our purpose. Considering that, what you do you believe your purpose is?

-

-

Chapter 2

Lying

Growing up in my house, there were certain things that were considered "no-no's," and I knew exactly what they were. In other words, there wasn't a lot of gray area. You knew exactly where the boundaries were, and you knew there were consequences of going outside of those boundaries. Dad always had a way of turning my mistakes into learning experiences. This was out of his desire for me not to repeat them over and over.

One nonnegotiable no-no was when I acted disrespectfully toward my mother. Dad would say, "That's your mom, but that's also *my wife*. You mess with her and you're messing with *me*." Another nonnegotiable no-no was lying. If you lied, you had to face the consequences. And the consequences were always the same . . . a spanking.

Yep. I know. There are some who don't believe in that type of punishment. I'm not here to debate that. My dad firmly (and I do mean *firmly*) believed in it. He never saw it as something he did to me. He always framed it as something I chose to receive by my own actions. Personal responsibility was never abdicated.

One particular day, when I was about five or six years old, I lied to my mom. She knew it. I was busted. I knew it. Then I yelled at her about it. If you weren't paying attention earlier, that's a double whammy. I lied *and* disrespected her.

Mom calmly looked at me and said, "Go to your room and wait for your father to get home."

That was the *worst*. Sitting in a room while you wait on the impending tornado of doom about to sweep into your space and fall upon your head is one of the most sickening feelings a kid can have.

Dad got home about thirty minutes after my mom sent me to my room. It felt like three hours. I heard the door. This was (obviously) before the days of cell phones, and I had to listen to my mother recount the details of my lying and disrespect to my father. After hearing about my misbehavior from my mother, it was now my father's duty to carry out my punishment.

About five minutes after he got home, I heard his feet clomping up the hall and, like a scene from a horror movie, watched the doorknob slowly turn to open as Dad entered my room. He looked at me with a stern glare. He closed the door behind him, crossed his arms, and said, "Well. Tell me what you did."

I looked at him and weakly replied, "I was disrespectful to Mom."

"What else?"

I looked down and said, "I lied."

"Well, Son, what happens when you lie?"

I kept staring downward and replied, "You get a spanking." And then I blurted out, "But I don't want one! Please don't spank me."

Dad sat there and stared at me.

I weakly said again through a couple of tears trickling down my face, "Please don't spank me. I won't do it again." (In actuality, this was probably the twentieth time I had lied about something.)

After a silence that felt like an eternity, Dad said, "Son, I'm not going to spank you. But I want you to know something: I'm extremely disappointed in you."

"I'm sorry, Dad. I won't do it again."

He replied, "Okay. Take off."

I wiped my face and got up and walked around him. As my hand reached the doorknob, I felt a swipe on my rear end, accompanied by a loud pop. It was hard enough that it slightly picked me up off the ground. I felt the unmistakable sting on my hind end. I turned and looked at him with a mixture of shock and betrayal on my face.

Dad looked me in the eye and said, "Son . . . *that's* what it feels like to be lied to."

That lesson stayed with me for the rest of my life. I'll confess, I even used it on one of my kids who had a bit of trouble with the truth at an early age in their life. I learned an extremely important lesson that day: tell the truth. Even when it hurts. Tell it. Don't run from it. Embrace it. A lie is merely delaying the inevitable pain as well as simultaneously increasing the pain of it.

Leadership Lesson: The short-term pain of the truth is infinitely better than living a long-term lie in misery. Tell the truth. Period.

APPLICATION:

- Do you need to make anything right with somebody? It's never too late to do the right thing. Do it today.

-

-

- Resolve to tell the truth—even when it hurts.

-

-

Chapter 3

Tomatoes

Growing up on a Missouri farm, Dad loved to grow things. Our backyard in Jackson, Tennessee, was large and would've been an ideal play area, but *no* . . . it was a garden. A garden I learned how to till and cultivate with my dad. I didn't like digging up the ground and working the soil. As an eight-year-old, working in a garden was not high on my priority list. Also, not all the vegetables being grown were ones I wanted to eat.

I knew planting squash meant there was a squash casserole in my near future, and for me, that was not a pleasant prospect. Yuck! (I know, some of you think I'm crazy.) Lima beans? No. To this day—*no*. Corn on the cob was good. I did enjoy that occasionally.

But there were two things I absolutely loved in that garden: cucumbers and tomatoes. I would peel those cucumbers and eat them like bananas. They were fresh and wonderful.

The tomatoes were a different thing. I loved fresh, homegrown tomatoes and still do. But what we had to go through to get them . . .

Tomatoes grow on the vine, and for those who don't know—they're green. They don't turn red until the very end.

And then there were the tomato worms. Those things have horns—so help me . . . *horns*. You know they're from the devil. Seriously. Google those suckers and tell me they're not some of the ugliest things you've ever seen. They're grotesque, huge, and they have to be removed from the plants with pliers. That's how strong their grip was. Okay, maybe I just didn't want to touch them, but either way, they had a strong grip, and it took pliers for me to get them off the plants.

Knowing how grossed out I was by the worms, Dad would send me out there with a pair of pliers and a smile to pull these demons off the plants so they wouldn't destroy all our tomatoes. As I was bent over dealing with these demonic worms from hell, Dad's greatest delight was to sneak up behind me and goose me, which sent me jumping six feet away; as a result, I would get very angry—which, of course, only made him laugh harder.

It would take the tomatoes we planted about two months (give or take some weeks) to grow. As they grew larger, I would want to pick them, but Dad would say, "No. It's not time. Don't take it too early. It'll be bad."

Patience wasn't and still isn't one of my virtues.

As the weeks progressed, I would see streaks of red on the tomatoes and would ask if I could pick it. "No, Son. You can't take it yet. It's not ready. It won't taste right. You have to let it ripen."

One day when we were in the garden, Dad saw me looking at a tomato, and he said, "You can go ahead and pick that one." From my vantage point, I could clearly see a green streak in the back of it.

I replied, "No, Dad. This one still has a green streak here."

He calmly instructed, "Go ahead and take it. You don't want to leave it on there too long. It'll spoil. It's ready."

So, I picked it and proudly held it up. Then Dad said this to me, "When it's green, it's growing, but when it's ripe—it's next to rotten. The same thing is true of you. Don't ever think you know it all. Keep learning. Be a student all of your life."

"When it's green it's growing, but when it's ripe—it's next to rotten. The same thing is true of you."

I have never met a person who "knows everything" and is successful. Period.

Leadership Lesson: You never arrive. You never know it all. School doesn't end when you graduate. It actually just begins.

APPLICATION:

- What areas of your life do you need to have more growth? Rate yourself on a scale from 1 to 10 in the following areas:

Spiritual _____

Mental _____

Emotional _____

Physical _____

Financial _____

- What areas need the most attention? Create a plan to start improving in those areas today.

-

-

Chapter 4

People

My dad's office at the college was often like a revolving door. Students, faculty, administrators, and prospective students provided a steady stream of visitors whenever he was in his office. For the administrators, he was a source of calming during conflicts. He was widely known at the college as a peacemaker. For the faculty, he was a source of knowledge for those seeking greater ways to relate to other faculty and the students. For those students, he was a source of wisdom. For some, he was another father. For a few, he was the only father figure they had. Thus, growing up around the college campus, I witnessed the seemingly never-ending line of visitors and occasionally was the secondhand beneficiary of his wisdom.

There were some gems I overheard:

"You're better than that, and I expect more of out you."

"Why would you settle for less than you know you're worth?"

"Get your wits about you."

"A dog can always beat a skunk, but it's never worth it."

"If you can't laugh at yourself, you're really missing the joke."

Sayings like these were wonderful to witness, but perhaps the greatest lesson I learned in Dad's office encounters was when people entered who were—let's just say—*not* happy. Dad would politely ask me to excuse myself, but not before I heard someone start ranting about an issue or problem they had with my father or with someone else.

I cannot tell you how many times I heard someone go into the office and say, "I can't believe you made me do this!" And after that, I often heard that same person exit the office ten minutes later saying something along the lines of "Dr. Hartley, thank you so much for letting me do this."

Dad was truly a master with people. I was always amazed at his people skills. I wish I had those skills. Make no mistake about it; he wasn't manipulative. He was a master at understanding others and helping them understand each other. He just knew and understood people. Today, we have loads of studies on IQs and EQs. There are personality evaluations based on DISC, Enneagrams, and Myers Briggs, to name a few. My dad never took any of those courses or evaluations. He was simply an incredible listener, and that skill empowered him to know the needs of others.

I witnessed one of these "confrontational" encounters upon entering my dad's office one day. This was after my decision to work in full-time ministry. Dad looked up at me as the person left the office and said, "Son, I want you to remember—ministry is 20 percent about skill and 80 percent about people. Get to know the people. Get to know what they are really saying. What do they need? Then find a way to meet those needs. Never go in with your hands out wanting something. Always go in with the intention of listening before you talk and meeting those needs."

A few years later, when I was working full time in a church, I was dealing with a particularly rude and rough person who told me I was too focused on myself and not focused enough on other people's needs. I told Dad what had happened, and he said, "Yeah, ministry would be great if it weren't for people."

Hold on! I thought. *You told me before that ministry was 80 percent about the people.* He could see the confusion on my face and realized I was missing the sarcasm.

Dad simply asked, "Son, do you think there is any truth in what the man was saying? I'm not saying the *way* he said it was right, but could there be any truth in what he told you?"

I lowered my head and thought for a moment, then answered, "Yeah. Maybe."

"Son, nobody is interested in building what you want. People will only follow you as far as it benefits and helps them. I know that sounds selfish, but to be a leader you have to meet people at *their* needs before you ever express your own. If you'll listen to their suggestions, meet their needs, and put their needs before your own, they'll follow you through fire. But if they feel like you're simply using them to get what you want, they won't cross the street for you."

"To be a leader you have meet people at their needs before you ever express your own."

I heard Zig Ziglar say it another way a few years later when I met him. "You can have everything you want in life if you'll just help enough people get what they want."[1]

Too many times in my early working life, I had a strong tendency to use people and love things. That is a recipe for disaster and a quick road to having zero influence. The opposite is true. One of the measures of a person is how they treat someone who can do absolutely nothing for them in return.

People are made to be empowered and loved. Things are made to be used and discarded. As leaders, we should never confuse the two.

Leadership Lesson: Love people. Use things. Meet people's needs before you express your own. Listen before you try to be heard. Your life's work is 80 percent people and 20 percent skill.

APPLICATION:

- Think about the people you influence and lead. What are their needs?

-

-

- If you don't know their needs, make it a point to find out this week.

-

-

- If you do know their needs, what are some steps, as a leader, you can take to meet those needs?

-

CHAPTER 5

THE LAWN MOWER

I loved seeing my grandmother during the summer, but there was one part I always dreaded: the lawn mower. My grandmother lived on about two acres of land outside of Joplin, Missouri, near the Oklahoma state line. Part of her lawn grew fairly slowly. Another part of the lawn looked like it was a mixture of cornstalks, wheat, and grass.

Okay, it was all grass and weeds, but to a kid, it was every bit as tall as corn. I could play hide-and-seek in it without ducking down.

Exploring Grandmother's property was always an adventure, but the property had to be mowed when we got there, and only one thing stood between us and the lawn being mowed . . . a vintage lawn mower.

This thing was a tractor ordered from Sears, Roebuck and Company sometime between the Civil War and the Vietnam War. I wasn't sure when. It was held together by paper clips and duct tape in a few places. That's not made up either. Literally paper clips and duct tape.

And so—when it was time to mow, I would go into the garage, push the lawn mower out, clean off all the cobwebs, and stand by and occasionally hand my dad tools, while he changed the oil and spark plugs, emptied the gas tank, put more gas in, and then cranked that sucker up only to be majorly disappointed when nothing happened.

Yeah, we replaced the battery too. No go.

Dad would get the instruction manual (written on Egyptian papyrus) and pore over it until he found a probable reason to explain why it wasn't starting, then off to Sears we'd go for replacement parts. Who knows what was wrong with this thing? Carburetor, timing belt, flux capacitor . . . I really had no clue. I know that if it could've generated 1.21 gigawatts, and I could have gone back in time with it, I'd have stopped my grandmother from buying it in the first place. I mean neither Mr. Sears, Mr. Roebuck, nor even Doc Brown could've salvaged this thing.

It was an old blue-and-white contraption. I actually looked it up on the internet, and for those who value technical things, it was a Sears Hydro-Trac 12. I was also fascinated to learn that some of them are still in circulation today and working quite well. Evidently, my grandmother's tractor was not that lucky.

Dad changed a belt on the side of the mower and managed to get the thing sputtering. White smoke billowed out of the exhaust in a large plume that would've made any cigar aficionado jealous. After about a thirty-second struggle for life, it died . . . again.

Fast forward three more hours, and it was finally determined the gas line was clogged. Dad fixed it, and the mower finally ran. Next up was a two-hour excursion in mowing the yard. You had to go super slow to get through the tall grass.

When I was under ten, it was thrilling to ride in my dad's lap and steer the tractor around. When I turned twelve, Dad turned me loose to mow the property myself. That was fun until I was about sixteen. Then it wasn't. Maybe it was because, by then, I had my own lawn-mowing business and was constantly mowing yards for six months out of the year.

It wasn't until I was out of college that I fully understood what Grandmother's whole lawn-mower business was about. First, it was about helping my elderly grandmother. I watched my father honor his mother by serving her. Second—and it was something I was too obtuse to get—it was about spending time with *me*.

Dad valued quality time with the family. It was his love language. For him, quality time meant interaction. It meant learning. It meant memories. My mind raced back to all the times we'd had together, including riding to different places where he had speaking or singing engagements, going to baseball games, riding rides together at amusement parks, and going to the World's Fair in 1982.

One particular experience stood out in my memory: my dad took our college singing group to New York City to sing in Lincoln Center. Another college from our town also attended, and a girl I was interested in was there. Instead of going on a Hudson River cruise on the same ship as my father, I decided to go on the ship with the girl. I watched from that ship as my dad's group (obviously without me) sang the national anthem from the ship directly in front of the Statue of Liberty. It was a precious moment in time that would never come again—and I missed it. I've regretted that to this day. Dad, of course, was gracious about it, but I think it bugged him too.

When I became a dad, my firstborn, a girl, was the apple of my father's eye. When she was a toddler, one of her favorite activities was going into Granddad's garden (that I mentioned in a previous chapter) and picking the big green peppers. She loved it. There was only one problem: those peppers were seasonal, not year-round. Of course, a toddler doesn't understand that at all, and she always expected to pick the peppers at his house. That's just something you did at Granddad's house.

Whenever Dad knew we were coming to his house, he would go to the grocery store, buy some large green peppers, and then individually tie them to a bush or tree so my daughter could pick them. She's over thirty years old today, but she still remembers picking peppers with Granddad.

Dad valued memories and experiences. Dad valued family. And Dad took care of his mother and others who could not take care of themselves.

Today, I try to do the same thing. I try to give my children and grandchildren memorable experiences. Those are the things that last. And it doesn't have to be elaborate. You just have to look for them. Sometimes, the most memorable experiences happen in a quiet conversation on a back porch or on an evening walk. Time spent with your loved ones is time well spent. I've attended hundreds of funerals, but I haven't attended one yet where they wished they had worked harder. I have, however, attended many where the family wished they had spent more time with their loved one before they passed.

You can schedule time with your loved ones just like you schedule meetings in your day. Make it an unbreakable appointment. People will understand. And if they don't, it's still okay. Schedule it anyway.

I've met many extremely wealthy individuals who had no relationship with their families. This is a tragic thing, but it's also very avoidable by intentionally making time for them. They should know they are the priority in your life, and your schedule should reflect that truth.

If you have significant others in your life, spend time with them today. Focus on making memories. It's not about the money you spend. It's about the time you invest.

> **"It's not about the money you spend.
> It's about the time you invest."**

Leadership Lesson: Time invested with your loved ones is time well spent. Spend time with them today and make those memories. If there is someone who cannot take care of themselves, invest some time and value in them today too.

APPLICATION:

- Are you scheduling time with the most important people in your life? Make some unbreakable appointments on your calendar this week.

-

-

Chapter 6

A Pound and a Half of Roast

My first job (besides my lawn-mowing business) was working in a grocery store named E. W. James and Sons in Jackson, Tennessee. I was a bag boy. I enjoyed that part because I liked interacting with the customers, and I often got pretty good tips. One of my jobs I didn't care for (besides mopping the aisles) was facing everything. For those who don't know, facing means you go through the entire store and take all the areas where customers have taken items off of the shelves and move what is toward the back of the shelves to the very front to make them look full. It was a tedious, time-consuming, pedantic job.

My least favorite aisle was the canned spaghetti and pizza sauce aisle because inevitably someone would knock off a bottle of pasta sauce, and it would shatter and splatter everywhere. Thus, I had to complete the dreaded task of mopping up the mess. My second least favorite aisle was the canned vegetables. It would take a lot of time to face that aisle, and it was always tedious, boring work.

On one occasion, I was facing cans on the canned vegetable aisle, and I decided to speed up my normal pace to see how fast I could get it done. While I successfully moved all the cans and stacked them toward the front of the shelves, I neglected to turn the labels toward the front where the customers could see them. No big deal, right? *Wrong*. My boss reprimanded me, saying, "How are they supposed to see what they're buying without being able to read the labels, Hartley? Do it over and do it *right* this time." And so, reluctantly, and perhaps saying a few choice words under my breath, I redid the entire aisle. What I thought would be a time-saver turned into double-time work.

When Dad picked me up from work (I was still under the legal age for driving) he could see my frustration. I relayed what had happened. He asked what he normally asked, "What did you learn from that?"

Feeling frustrated, I replied, "My boss is pretty obsessive when it comes to the canned vegetable aisle," in a smart-alecky tone.

Dad furrowed his brow and instantly replied, "Son, this wasn't your boss's fault. It was yours. Let me tell you a story."

(*Here we go,* I thought with an internal eye roll.)

I never knew my dad's father. He passed away four years before I was born. So, everything I knew about him came from stories from my grandmother, my parents, and other relatives. I knew he and my grandmother ran a local grocery store in Joplin, Missouri. It was a small grocery store, where people came in, told them what they wanted at the counter, and my grandparents assembled their order into grocery bags and handed it to them over the counter. It was Insta-Cart without the home delivery! My dad and his siblings worked in that grocery store during their teenage years as butchers. So, understanding all of that, Dad relayed the following story:

My uncle Howard was working at the store late one evening, and as they were about to close, in walked Mrs. Potter. She was known for coming in at the last minute and demanding lots of things. That night, she wanted some roast beef. Because it was so near closing, Howard had already put up almost all the meat in the freezer, except for a little less than one pound of roast that remained in the meat cabinet.

Mrs. Potter looked at Howard and said, "I'd like a pound of roast."

Howard knew if Mrs. Potter wanted more than what he had underneath that counter, it meant going back into the freezer, pulling out a slab of meat, cutting it for her, and then having to clean up again, which at this point in the day, he didn't want to do. He pulled out the roast he had from below the counter and showed her. She scratched her chin and asked, "Do you have anything else?" Not wanting to have to go back into the freezer, Howard realized that if he flipped the roast over, it actually looked a little larger on the other side. So, he took the piece of meat and lowered it behind the counter as if he were picking up some more, but instead, he just flipped it over and squished it around until it formed a different shape. After that, he brought it back into view and said, "How about this one?"

Mrs. Potter thought for a moment and then said, "I'll tell you what. I'll take both of them."

Howard dropped his head, went back to the freezer, and did what he should have done the first time—be up front and honest.

Then Dad looked at me and said, "Son, always do the right thing the first time. It doesn't just save time; it also builds your character."

Leadership Lesson: If you already know how, do it the right way the first time. Don't cut corners. Be up front. Be honest. It saves time and builds your character.

APPLICATION:

- Are there areas of your life where you're taking the easy way out, instead of doing things the right way the first time? What are some areas you know you could improve in by not cutting any corners?

-

-

Chapter 7

Expectations

Sally was a chronic complainer. I was leading a volunteer group (which, by the way, is a great test of your leadership skills), and she always had something to say. Sometimes, what she said was public in front of everyone; other times, it was behind the scenes, like a torpedo in the water, waiting to hit the hull of my "leader ship" and sink it.

I did nice things for Sally and her family. I thought that might help.

It didn't.

She continued to complain. She complained to other people. She complained in front of our group. She complained to whomever would listen.

I couldn't understand what I had done to inspire such dislike in her, but I finally asked politely for her to stop saying negative things in front of our group. I told her it was disruptive to others and disrespectful to me.

She stopped talking in front of everyone and began acting passive aggressively angry in our group time. And she escalated her behind-the-scenes complaining. More and more people were coming to me, telling me things Sally had said.

I began to take a lot of this very personally and met with my dad to tell him what was going on. He listened intently as I ranted and raved for about fifteen minutes solid about how irritating and disappointing she was. I also called her a backstabber because of all I'd done for her.

When I finally ran out of steam, Dad asked, "Is that it?"

"Yes, sir. I guess that's it."

"How do you feel right now?" Dad probed a little further.

I thought for a few seconds, then replied, "It's a mixture of irritation and disappointment, I guess."

"Let me make sure I understand this: this lady complains all the time."

"Yes."

"She complains consistently?"

"Yes, sir. All the time."

"She's never positive?"

"Maybe once or twice."

"So, she's a chronic complainer?"

"Yes! I've said that three times now. Why do you keep asking me?"

"And she has really disappointed you?"

"Yes!"

"And you feel you deserve to be treated better than she is treating you?"

"*Yes!*" I was irritated.

Dad sat back in his chair and said, "I can tell you exactly what the problem is."

I leaned forward, waiting to catch this nugget of wisdom. "Okay, what is it?"

Dad looked into my eyes and calmly replied, "You."

"Me? What did I do?"

"Son, if this woman complains all the time like you say, then why in the world would you be disappointed when she complained some more? It seems like the problem isn't in the woman's complaints. The problem is in your expectations."

I was frustrated with him now.

"Son, if I know a person is a liar, I expect them to lie. If I know they are cheaters, I expect them to cheat. If this woman is a chronic complainer, then you should expect her to complain. You'll never be disappointed again. When someone shows you who they are, Son, believe it. Complaining about her is like complaining about the rain. You can do it, but what's the point? Isn't it better to just grab an umbrella and go with it?"

I replied, "You mean accept what it is and adjust my expectations and my attitude accordingly?"

"Exactly!" he answered. "Grab your umbrella and go on, and eventually you'll find the fair weather."

> "Everyone complains about the weather, but nobody does anything about it." —Mark Twain

Dad continued, "There are two ways to go through life. In expectation of the way you feel people should be and in expectation of how everyone should treat you, *or* . . . you can simply accept people as they are and realize that the only person you can affect change in is yourself. I'm not saying not to hope for the best in people. It's fine to hope for the best in people, but you can't expect it. Expectation and hope are two very different things. Expectations are dependent on other people's actions. Hope is dependent upon *you* and your own attitudes and beliefs."

"The only person you can affect change in is yourself."

When we expect things from people, that leads us to disappointments. In fact, that's what a disappointment is: an unmet expectation. If we live life expecting others to treat us a certain way, we are setting ourselves up to be disappointed because, ultimately, we cannot control what others say about us or how they treat us. We can never control the actions or words of other people, and that is the very essence of expectation. We cannot be responsible for what they say and do. We can only be responsible for how we respond to them. It is an exercise in futility to fret over what we cannot control.

When we live by expectations, we are giving the keys to our emotions to other people to drive. When we accept people and things the way they are, we live in reality and maintain hope in our hearts and minds that if *we* treat people better, then it will be reciprocated sometimes and even life-changing for others.

> *"Be the change you want to see in the world."* —Mahatma Ghandi

Leadership Lesson: Lay aside expectations of everyone except yourself. They lead us to disappointment because they are dependent on the actions of others. Embrace people and things the way they are—and keep the hope alive that if you improve and treat others the way *you* would want to be treated, then you can change the world.

APPLICATION:

- Who has recently disappointed you? Was that a result of their actions only, or was it a result of your expectations of them? Maybe a combination of both?

-

-

- Thinking about them, were their actions consistent with who they are?

-

-

- Could an adjustment in your expectations ease your disappointment?

-

-

Chapter 8

Reader's Digest Critics

At first, it was one person who "wanted to bring some issues to my attention." Then it was three. Then five or six. What started as one complaint had turned into a steady stream and I wanted to know why.

I felt many of the complaints were without merit. I felt they were distracting me and other good people from the goals we had set. My leadership position seemed to be hanging by a thread.

So, by the time I got to Dad to ask him what to do, I was pretty frustrated and a little scared. I explained the situation to him.

He asked, "Is this just one group of people coming to you?"

I thought for a moment, then replied, "No. It seems to be coming from two or three."

"Who is the common denominator?" he inquired.

"What do you mean?" I asked.

"If there are two or three groups complaining, always look for the common denominator. There will always be one or maybe two people who are present in all the groups."

As soon as he said it, I knew. It was John.

John was a politician. Oh, maybe not in the most literal sense. He didn't hold any public office in our district, but he was constantly lobbying for his own preferences.

John's preferred approach did not include telling you straight to your face either. He would make his wishes known to others and then get them to approach someone for him, as if it were their own opinion. He stirred the pot from behind the scenes.

After Dad asked me the common denominator question, I instantly realized that John was a part of each of the groups that was complaining. After this epiphany, I thanked Dad and told him I was all too ready to rip John's head from atop his shoulders, but Dad said, "Hang on a second. Let's just talk about this."

I sat and waited for him to say what I most likely didn't want to hear.

"Son, let's look at what these complaints are. Take the emotion out of it for a minute and ask yourself, 'Is there *any* truth to what these people are saying?'"

As much as I hated to admit it, there was some truth to it. I immediately got defensive and said, "But they're also saying things that are *not* true, and I need to go confront this!"

Dad—ever the calm, collected peacemaker—simply replied, "You've got to approach this like a *Reader's Digest*."

For those who have zero clue what *Reader's Digest* is, it is a magazine (online now) that came every month with a compilation of interesting, newsworthy, humorous, and even poignant articles assembled from media sources from all over the world. Today, we have the internet to give us those highlights, but back then, it was *Reader's Digest*.

When my father told me to approach the situation like I was reading a *Reader's Digest*, I understood the meaning behind his statement immediately. Nobody ever sat down and read a *Reader's Digest* from cover to cover. You simply picked the articles that appealed to you and discarded the rest.

I looked at Dad, realizing, and replied, "So I need to accept the truth that is inside the criticism and discard the rest."

Dad smiled and said, "Yep. That's what I'd do. Son, you're going to find in every bit of criticism, no matter how unfair or how personal the attack, there is always some tinge of truth. If you can grab that truth and set aside the rest, you'll get better, you'll grow stronger, and you'll learn and improve, while avoiding becoming defensive and bitter."

"You're going to find in every bit of criticism, there is always some tinge of truth."

His point was well taken. But I also asked, "What about my 'common denominator'?"

"How much time have you spent talking to this guy and finding out what he really wants?"

I admitted that it wasn't much. I mean, who would want to talk to a guy like that? I felt I had better things to do with my time!

"Why don't you give it a shot and get back with me on that one."

I did *not* want to do this. I was upset at the guy for undermining my leadership. I didn't want to be around him, much less talk with him. But I knew my father's wisdom and trusted his advice, so I did it.

John was shocked to get my phone call. When we sat down together for lunch, he was immediately defensive. I just said, "John, I wanted to have lunch with you today to get to know you, to see how you're doing, and to get your input on any ideas you might have."

I saw a change in his countenance immediately.

For the next thirty minutes, I listened to John unload some of his criticisms and ideas about our organization. And here's the thing: there were some good ideas there. I had to make myself look past the critical comments and what I perceived were personal attacks (more on that in a later chapter) and really listen to what he was saying.

After he was done unloading, I said, "John, you know—you have some really good ideas here. I really appreciate you sharing them with me."

John looked like he'd been slapped. After a little more small talk, he opened up to me about some deep personal problems he was having. After listening to him for another ten minutes or so, I realized many of his complaints had nothing to do with me. They were related to his personal issues. I looked him in the eyes and listened to him. Then I told him I had heard what he'd said. He thanked me, and we parted ways.

I thought quite a bit about that "Reader's Digest." John had a few good articles, but there were obviously deeper issues there that had nothing to do with me. There was one idea he had that I knew I could and would implement that would greatly improve our communication. I started planning for it, but here's the thing: before I could ever implement that idea, John suddenly became one of my greatest advocates. My common denominator critic had turned into a cheerleader for me and my leadership *before* I had made any changes.

When I relayed this information to Dad, he simply said, "Son, always remember, sometimes people just want to be heard. Once they know you care enough to listen to them, they'll follow you."

Per usual, Dad was right.

As I was leaving after this huge lesson, Dad dropped another bomb on me. "One more thing, Son. Always remember this: if you're looking for that common denominator and can't find it, consider that the common denominator may be *you*. Look at yourself for correction before you look at others. Listen to their needs before you express your own."

Leadership Lesson: If you're experiencing a lot of problems, always look for the common denominator. If you can't seem to find the common denominator, consider that it might be you. Approach criticism like it's a *Reader's Digest*. Take the truth (articles), discard the rest, and realize in the process that some critics simply want to be heard. Listen to them, and you may just find that your critic can become a cheerleader.

APPLICATION:

- Think about any complaints you've been fielding. Is there *any* truth in them?

-

- Did the common denominator idea resonate with you? Did somebody come to mind?

-

- Write out some ways you could possibly connect with your common-denominator person.

-

Chapter 9

Mr. Fix It

In the 1983 movie *A Christmas Story*, there is a scene where they are lighting the Christmas tree in their living room. "The Old Man Parker" has six or seven plugs in the same outlet, and he blows a fuse. You hear him call out in the darkness: "Hold it right there! A fuse is out!" The narrator and writer, Jean Shepherd, then says, "The old man could replace fuses quicker than a jackrabbit on a date. He bought them by the gross."

That scene always makes me smile because it reminds me of my dad. He was truly "Mr. Fix It!" Unfortunately for me, that gene seems to have skipped a generation. Most of the repairs I do are done with a checkbook.

Dad carried a toolbox in the car. If something in the house was broken that he couldn't repair, he would sit there and say, "Just let me think about this for a minute." Somehow, he knew if he calmly and carefully assessed the situation, then a solution would present itself, and eventually, it always did.

I believe that is part of my problem; Dad had a large amount of patience that also seems to have escaped me.

After I moved out, it was always great whenever Dad would visit my house. It seemed he instinctively knew what was broken in the house. In a matter of minutes, that tool kit would be in his hands and the repairs would commence.

From a leaking sink to loose screws, no piece of faulty hardware was safe from his repair skills. By the time he would leave the house, everything that was broken was fixed. He even upgraded things in the home and did other tasks, including hanging pictures.

The bottom line is when Dad came to our house, he always left things far better than he found them. I found out from other extended family members that he did the same thing for them. In fact, his desire to help others was a guiding principle in his life. When he encountered people, he constantly looked for ways he could help them and leave them better than when he found them.

One such person was Pam. She was a wonderful, beautiful young lady who entered the college where my dad taught. She was from a very small town and had little confidence in her skills. She received some scholarships for her musical abilities, but it wasn't enough to cover all of her expenses, and her family couldn't afford to cover the rest. She was facing having to quit college and go back home.

Dad saw all this going on and decided to do something about it. Dad immediately recognized her talents and abilities. Pam struggled with her self-confidence, but Dad spoke life into her by telling her he believed in her. But he didn't stop there. He came up with a plan with my mom to pay for Pam's college anonymously.

Pam ended up staying and finishing college. After graduation, she worked in Nashville at Opryland and did some nationwide commercials, including one with Loretta Lynn. She even appeared on stage with George Burns for a television special. She met a wonderful man, got married, and began writing music for children. Many of her publications gained national recognition and have even sold worldwide. Pam pours her life into children, carrying on the tradition of my father.

To this day (to my knowledge), Pam never knew that my father was the one who paid for her college. Pam couldn't repay what my dad had done, but it wasn't about repaying. He simply did what he always did—he added value to someone who could offer nothing in return. "Mr. Fix It" found a way to leave someone better than when he found them.

When you value other people and add value to them based on their needs, that is the essence of leaving them better than when you found them. That is leadership.

Leadership Lesson: Value other people. Find out what they value, then add value to them. Leave them better than they were when you first encountered them.

APPLICATION:

- Who can you add value to today who can do *nothing* for you in return?

-

-

- What are some things you can do for them?

-

-

- Do something for them . . . *today*.

-

-

Chapter 10

Motivation and Inspiration

As I established in an earlier chapter, I was a slacker for my first three semesters of college. For me, like many others, college represented my first excursion into my own independent choices. And wow! Did I screw it up! College wasn't a learning institution for me. It was a socialization outlet. Fraternities, parties, shooting pool, dates, conversations—okay—*anything* other than schoolwork was the priority.

Here's a little tidbit I haven't mentioned yet. I went to the college where my dad taught. I had him for some classes. So, there was no way to BS my way through classes. I still have some of my tests that he wrote across the top of them:

"Nice try."

"Next time, try studying the material."

"Show up for more classes and you'll probably improve."

You get the idea. . . .

Dad knew where my issues were before I ever got to college. He just watched me manifest on the outside what I had been sowing on the inside. I had breezed through high school graduating in the top 15 percent out of four hundred graduates. But here's the thing: I was barely even trying. I just didn't take it seriously.

One of my first music professors in college started our class by saying, "Welcome to college. If you show up, fine. If you don't show up, that's fine too. Either way, I don't care."

Hey! My kind of professor! Of course, he didn't mention that if I didn't show up, I also didn't pass. I just took it as permission to do what I wanted. And I did exactly that. I showed up (sometimes) for my classes. I studied occasionally (almost always the night before) for exams. And at the end of my first two collegiate semesters, my grades reflected my work ethic—1 A, 3 Cs, 2 Ds, and 1 big fat F.

Dad didn't freak out on me. He just asked me what I was doing. I replied, "I don't know. I'm just not motivated. I need to find the motivation to do better."

Rather than chastise me, Dad simply said, "You need to find it within yourself to do this or not. It's really your choice, Son. You're waiting for someone to come by and make you do better. I can tell you right now—that person isn't coming by. That person is *you*. Instead of looking for motivation, try inspiration."

I thought those were basically the same thing. My furrowed brow revealed my confusion, and Dad could always read me like a book.

He continued, "Motivation is based on external forces. People and circumstances that surround you can motivate or demotivate you. Inspiration comes from the inside. One is based on outside circumstances and people, and the other is based on *you*."

"Motivation is based on external forces. Inspiration comes from the inside."

I knew he was right. Nothing within my college environment was going to magically make me be on time (or show up!) for my classes. Nobody was coming alongside me to say, "Hey, Ken! Study!" Nothing in my surroundings was going to encourage me to put off temporary time wasters in favor of long-lasting success. I had to find something inside of me to get me going.

> "You keep waiting for someone to come by and turn you on. What if they don't show up?" —Jim Rohn

Great question. And Jim Rohn was right; nobody showed up.

Motivation is based on the Greek word *kine*, which means "in motion" (think kinetic energy). It is referring to forces around us that put us in motion in a certain direction. To expound on that a bit more—it's an outside force moving us in the direction it thinks we should go. But there is a catch: what if the direction that outside force is moving us in is *not* consistent with where we should be going?

That pretty much summed up my college career thus far. I was motivated all right! I was just motivated in the *opposite* direction of where I should have been going!

Inspiration at its root meaning is "in spirit," which means it comes from inside of our spirits. It is something that happens on the inside of us that eventually manifests on the outside. Most of the time, observers cannot even tell there's a difference in us when true inspiration hits. But eventually, what is on the inside will make its way to the outside *if we cultivate it*.

Leadership Lesson: Motivation is based on outside influences. Inspiration comes from inside us. We are not in control of motivation. We are very much in control of inspiration. Pour into yourself and be inspired to do and be more today.

APPLICATION:

- What specific steps are you taking today to inspire yourself?

-

-

- What are you reading and/or listening to on a daily basis?

-

-

- Don't think in terms of the time it takes to do this. It's not about the time. It's much more about small things done *consistently*.

-

-

Chapter 11

The Fishing Pole in the Corner

I've given you some of my father's wisdom in the last several chapters. Dad had a way of saying and doing things where you didn't forget them. But not all the memories were positive ones.

Right after Dad's funeral, my siblings and I started the difficult process of cleaning out some of my father's possessions. I was tasked with cleaning out his tool shed. As I said in a previous chapter, he could fix anything. This, of course, meant he had a tool shed full of tools. "The right tool for the job makes it all easier," he would say.

When I saw the movie *Gran Torino*, with Clint Eastwood, there was a scene in his garage where you can see all the elderly man's tools on the wall. That setup reminded me of Dad's tool shed, only Clint's was more organized. Dad's shed was organized—to him and *only* him. To the average person, it looked like a mess of tools and oil cans stacked up randomly, but you didn't dare move anything around because he knew exactly where things were in the clutter.

I began sorting through all the tools. My brother wanted most of them, and I was happy to oblige. It's not as if I knew how to use them. As I cleaned out more and more, something in the corner caught my eye. It was a brand-new fishing pole and a new tackle box. When I say new, I mean the price stickers were still on them.

Dad bought them the week before he retired from teaching college. He loved to fish. My thoughts went back to a few of our fishing excursions together. I remembered the first time he taught me how to hook a worm on the end of my line. I remember the first fish "I caught" and how "we" reeled him in. I remember him teaching me how to clean a fish I'd caught. I remember the tranquil moments sitting on the banks of a pond in central Missouri, listening to the willows blow in the wind and hearing the fish jump in the pond. They were such great memories. He didn't get to fish very much, but I know he loved it.

Dad bought the fishing gear in anticipation of his retirement and finally having time to fish. He was diagnosed with stomach cancer about a month after he retired, and the pole, bait, and tackle box all sat in that corner untouched for almost two years until I found them.

The lesson screamed out at me. That fishing pole represented something he loved to do that he never did. It represented tranquil days on the water that never were. It represented rest and relaxation for him.

There were moments at the college when he was under incredible stress and conflict that would've caused others to crumble; however, I believe that the stress in his life caused his stomach ulcers that later turned into cancer. I couldn't help but wonder at times if a few more trips out the door with that fishing pole could have remedied the stress of his job. It's always easy to ask yourself "what if" after the fact. That can become an exercise in futility, so we won't do that.

I began to think about the trips I didn't take with the family because I was "so busy" or because there were things I "had to take care of." A hard truth about my job hit me between the eyes: I could work as hard as I could at a job all of my life and be replaced in a heartbeat. I might be missed for a short season, but those I worked with would soon forget me, and everyone would just go about their lives as if I never even existed.

Or there was a better option for my life; I could spend time with my loved ones who would remember those moments as vividly as I remember my moments with my father. I made a decision that day to spend time with my family. I decided I wouldn't wait to take that vacation. I decided it was perfectly acceptable and *even spiritual* to take that day off and get away to rest. I made a choice; and to this day, I have never regretted it.

There will come a day when you won't be able to tell that special person face-to-face what they have meant to you. There will come a day when the petty differences you've had won't be nearly as aggravating as you thought they were. Not to be morbid here, but truthful—staring at a coffin or a gravestone can put things into perspective pretty quickly. Whatever you need to say to that loved one, do it today. Tomorrow is not promised to anyone.

There was a movie that came out several years ago called *The Bucket List*, starring Jack Nicholson and Morgan Freeman as two aging, terminally ill men. Jack's character had loads of money and Morgan's character had great ideas and perspectives. They created a bucket list and set out to check off every item on their list. They spent their last days living life to its fullest. It's an entertaining and poignant story and a great reminder for all of us: do it today.

"Do it today."

Take that trip. Have that conversation. Go for that walk. Have that meal. Watch that sunset. Turn off that phone. Unplug that computer. Make new memories *today*. You are not promised tomorrow.

One of the saddest sights I ever saw was that brand-new fishing pole, unused in a corner. It represented unrealized potential. It represented some incredible days that never came to be.

Success and leadership are wonderful aspirations, but be sure you don't lose the important things along the way. There is still love to experience, memories to make and share, conversations to have, and life to live. Don't miss it!

Leadership Lesson: Do it. Do it now. Don't wait. If you need to have a conversation with someone about forgiveness or just to tell them you love them, don't wait. Say it today. Tomorrow may be too late. Don't get so caught up in planning life that you miss out on actually living it.

APPLICATION:

- You can always check your priorities by checking your calendar. How does your calendar look when compared with your priorities?

-

-

- What conversation(s) do you need to have today?

-

-

- What vacation have you been putting off because you're "too busy" or you "have to do" something?

-

-

- Is rest and rejuvenation built into your schedule on a weekly, monthly, and annual basis?

-

-

- Prioritize your rest so you'll be able to do more with your loved ones.

-

-

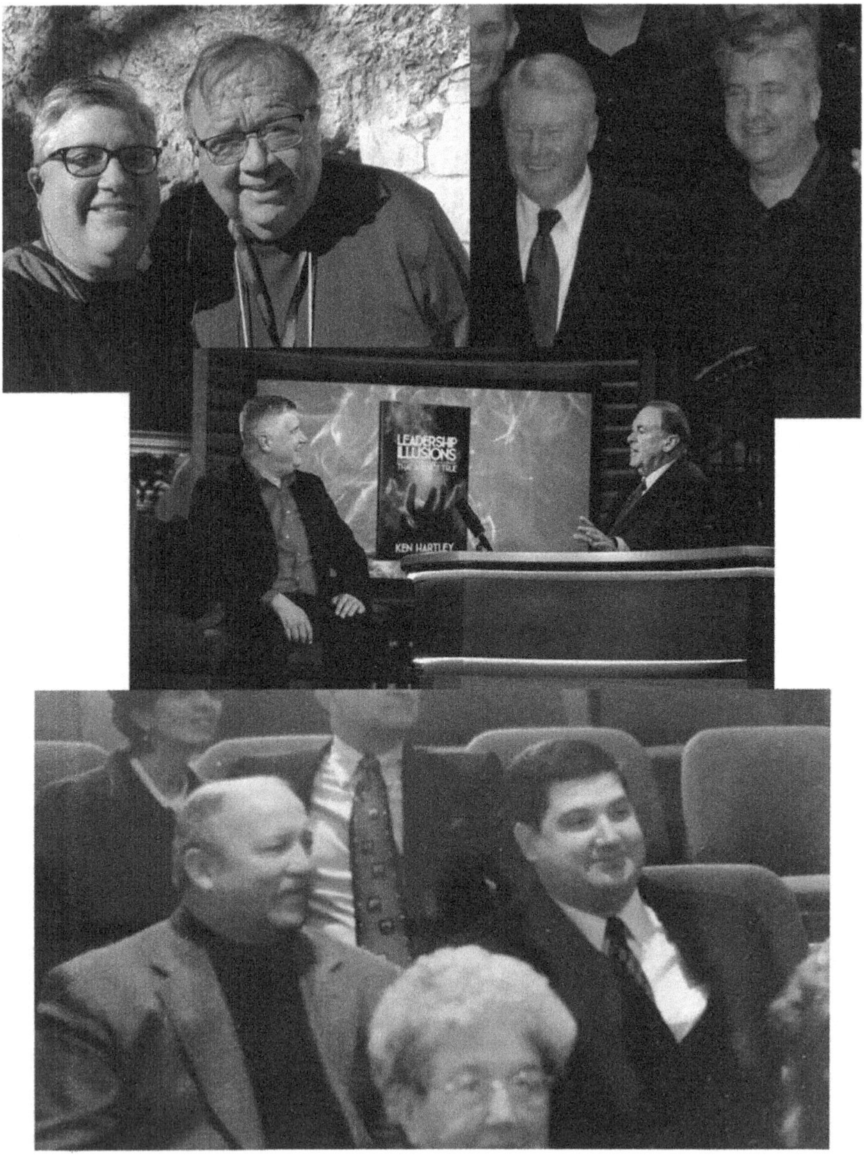
LEADERSHIP
ILLUSIONS
KEN HARTLEY

Section II

Spiritual Fathers

As you've read, my father was an extraordinarily wise person who constantly gave me wisdom and truth mixed with a large dose of love. I was incredibly blessed to have him in my life for thirty-two years. I have also been blessed to have spiritual fathers. While we aren't related by blood, we definitely shared kindred spirits—hence the name. They have given me the lessons, wisdom, and words of a father. I hope you'll learn as much from them as I have.

Part II

Dr. James D. Whitmire

Dr. Jim Whitmire was the minister of music at Bellevue Baptist Church in Memphis, Tennessee, when I met him. He grew one of the largest music ministries in the world and had a weekly attendance (in the music ministry alone, mind you) of over three thousand people. I attended one of his Christmas programs at the church and was absolutely blown away. I knew I had to get to know him and learn as much as I could from him. He was beyond gracious in sharing his wisdom, his skills, and most importantly, his time.

I've always been a believer in that if I wanted to know how to do something, I had to find someone who was already successfully doing it and learn as much as I possibly can from them. Success breeds success. I learned so much from Dr. Whitmire. Today, he still pours his life into music ministry students in a seminary in Memphis. He is an amazing man that hundreds of people in ministry have sought to imitate, both professionally and personally.

CHAPTER 12

HARD WORK AND FAILURE

On the invitation of a friend in college, I attended a performance of the "Singing Christmas Tree" at Bellevue Baptist Church in Memphis, Tennessee, in 1987. My home church had done a Christmas Tree program every year, so my thoughts about going to this program were, *Been there, seen it, done it.*

I was *so* wrong.

It was overwhelming. It was sensory overload. The orchestra played to perfection. They marched almost fifty intricately decorated banners that were all artistic masterpieces, easily worth $1,000 each. They had a handbell choir that played better than anything you've ever heard on TV. The acting and singing were on par with anything you'd see in New York City. I'm not kidding. I've seen many Broadway blockbusters, and the sets and production level of this was every bit as good. And I was in a *church*! I couldn't believe it!

I had to meet the guy who oversaw all of this, so I did. Jim Whitmire was extremely busy and couldn't talk to me, but I was determined to make an appointment with him later, which I did a few weeks after that performance. When I met with him, the drive from my college to the church took ninety minutes.

I was early for the meeting. I entered a modest office, and for the next forty-five minutes, I ran through a list of questions I had. I came prepared. I wanted to do what he was doing, and I had to know how he had done it. I didn't realize it at the time, but I was setting a pattern that I would follow for the rest of my life: when you know what you want to do, find someone who is doing it successfully (hopefully at the highest level) and enlist them to mentor you. Years later, I found out that Jim had been mentored by another music minister named John Gustavson in California.

As I sat there questioning Jim, I realized it would have taken a year of questioning to get the information I needed. Fortunately (for Jim), I didn't spend a year with him, but I did meet with him once a quarter for an hour each time. He was so gracious in giving his time and didn't have to do so.

In 1990, Jim gave me a very rare and rich offer. He gave me the chance to shadow him for a week prior to one of his large stage productions. I, of course, took the opportunity. There were tons of rehearsals, and I attended all of them without saying a word. I took lots of notes. One thing became perfectly clear to me after the first eleven-hour day. Jim worked hard. I mean *really* hard.

Every meeting had a purpose, and it all flowed toward the ultimate goal, but there was simply no substitute for all of his hard work. He had the right people in the right positions on his team, but there were certain tasks only he could and would do, and he did them all to perfection. He was surrounded by some of the most talented individuals I've ever seen. I knew there were parts of this he could have "phoned in", but instead, he pressed in more to make the production something exceptional. Good was never good enough for Jim Whitmire. Talent without hard work is a dime a dozen.

"Nothing in the world will take the place of persistence. Talent will not. The world is full of unsuccessful people with talent. Genius will not; unrewarded genius is almost a proverb. Education will not. The world is full of educated failures. Persistence and determination alone are omnipotent." —Calvin Coolidge[2]

"The world is full of unsuccessful people with talent. – Calvin Coolidge"

Hard work versus talent will win every time, but talent combined with hard work is absolutely unstoppable.

In one dress rehearsal, one part went terribly wrong. I knew how it was supposed to go because I was actually in the meeting where they discussed it. It was a scene depicting the crucifixion, and one of the people on one of the crosses almost fell off onto the floor in what could have been a serious injury. There were people in the audience for the rehearsal too. There were a few screams and gasps. Thankfully, the actor was not injured.

Jim didn't get upset. He simply had a *very* clear meeting after the dress rehearsal and made sure every member of the crew knew how that scene was supposed to go, and they introduced another safety feature to keep the actor safe. The next night (opening night) came off without a hitch, and that particular scene was one of the most moving and powerful scenes in the entire presentation.

I learned another important lesson that day. Jim never avoided something big for fear of failure. In fact, he seemed to embrace failure as his friend. He learned great lessons from it and grew stronger.

He told me, "Don't be afraid to try new things. There are lots of things I tried that didn't work, but I always learned something from them. If you have that attitude, the wrong ideas can lead you to some very good ones that will work. Nobody ever became successful without failing first. If you're going to be good at anything, you have to be willing to be bad at it at first."

Some of the first productions I did were bad. Very bad. As in, I'm surprised people in the audience didn't throw rotten tomatoes at me! But I learned from these failures. More on this in a later chapter....

Over the years, Jim and I cultivated not only a relationship of mentor/mentee, but we also became good friends. Those lessons have stayed with me, and I still use them to this day.

Leadership Lesson:

> 1. If you want to learn to do something, find someone already doing it and get them to mentor you. Pay them if you have to. The knowledge you will acquire will far outweigh the costs of learning it.
>
> 2. There is no substitute for hard work. Hard work beats talent every time. Talent combined with hard work, however, becomes an unstoppable force.

3. Embrace failure. It's a friend. Learn from it. The wrong ideas can lead you to good ones if you're willing to learn and grow.

APPLICATION:

- What did you fail at recently? (Here's a quick tip: if you haven't failed at anything recently, it's a good sign you haven't challenged yourself significantly.)

-

-

- What did you learn from it?

-

-

- What have you *not* tried because of your fear of failure?

-

-

- Set a date on your calendar now as a goal to do it!

-

-

CHAPTER 13

CHILDLIKE WONDER

I was with a group of creatives who were at a conference at the Walt Disney World Resort in Orlando, Florida. It was Disney's "Year of a Million Dreams," and they were doing things during that year they had never done (and have never since). I was on a bus with about forty other creatives, including Jim Whitmire, pulling into the Magic Kingdom.

The host from Disney on the bus was describing the "Year of a Million Dreams" and asking us what our Disney dream would be? Many passengers on the bus said they wanted to see the "Utilidors," also known as the lower level below the Magic Kingdom. In case you didn't know it, the Magic Kingdom has a system of tunnels underneath the level all of us walk on called "Utilidors" that Walt Disney himself designed to keep trash collection and cast members from various sections from having to walk through sections they shouldn't. In other words, it would look bad to see a cowboy from Frontierland walking through Tomorrowland and would make for a "bad show" for the guests.

The host was explaining this and several other things, and he asked again, "What would be your dream to see this year at Disney World?" Someone said, "The inside of the castle," to which they replied that random people were being chosen every day to spend the night there.

I was thinking about something I had always wanted to see. I am (by hobby) an illusionist and have performed stage illusions all over the world. There is a very old stage illusion that Professor Pepper developed in the late 1800s. Yes, he was really called Professor Pepper. The illusion would cause an apparent "ghost" to appear and disappear next to live actors on stage and was a sensation among theatergoers at that time. When Disney was developing the Haunted Mansion attraction at the parks, the lead developer, X Atencio, adopted this illusion and incorporated it into the attraction. The only modern-day application of Pepper's Ghost today is at the Disney parks.

So, when the host asked us about our dream, I wanted to see backstage at the Haunted Mansion, which is exactly what I asked for. The host grimaced a bit when I asked, and he replied, "Yeah, that's not really possible. I can basically tell you how the ghosts work, but I can't take you down there."

I smiled and replied, "I'm an illusionist. I already know how they work. I just wanted to see it up close and in action."

She smiled back and said, "I'm sorry."

The bus pulled up backstage at Main Street at the Magic Kingdom, and our big surprise that day was we were going to be given a tour of the Utilidors. I had already seen the tunnels, so it wasn't that big of a deal for me.

As I exited the bus, the host was standing on the ground outside of the bus directing people. She whispered to me as I stepped down, "Stand over there." My heart jumped a little bit, and I stood where she told me to stand.

Jim Whitmire was getting off the bus behind me, and he saw the exchange and asked, "What did she say?"

I told him, "She told me to stand here."

Jim said, "I'm going to stand here too."

The host turned to us and said, "If we do this, you'll miss seeing a lot of the Utilidors."

I replied, "I've already seen them," and Jim indicated the same thing.

She looked at us and said, "Can you both run?"

We replied almost in unison, "Yes!"

And off we went through a back entrance into the Magic Kingdom, in front of the castle, into a part of Fantasyland, and through a "cast members only" exit into a part I had never seen. We approached a large, warehouse-looking building, and we entered through a metal door, where we saw backstage at the Haunted Mansion. I saw the ghosts. It confirmed many of my guesses as to the details of how they worked. We stayed for about five minutes and then went back and rejoined our group. Most of them didn't have a clue that we got that backstage peek, and Jim and I never talked about it.

My dream was fulfilled. I got to see something most people will never get to see. As an illusionist, it was an extremely special memory. It was especially memorable, though, because I got to share it with my mentor. He exhibited a quality that I have attempted to hold on to my entire life: *childlike wonder and curiosity.*

Jim is always curious about how something works. He is constantly asking questions and learning. He is truly a lifelong student.

When I first started doing productions at the small church I was serving, I brought videos of those productions to Jim. I look back on it now and am embarrassed that I showed some of them to him. But here's the thing: Jim would intently watch my videos. And I don't mean he was being polite. He was *genuinely* interested. Yes, he gave me honest feedback, both good and bad, which was immensely helpful, but he went beyond that. He was actually looking at those videos for ideas . . . for things he didn't know about yet. And . . . he asked *me* questions and found a few ideas that he incorporated into his productions.

I heard him say more than once, "If there's something good there I can use, I will!" He was constantly searching for new and innovative ideas.

I attended a conference at Jim's church in the early '90s. He was teaching a seminar on doing productions and talked about always looking for new ideas. He singled me out in a group of about two hundred people as a person he got ideas from. I was shocked. I was in a church with barely a hundred people in attendance, and his church had thousands of members and unlimited resources. But Jim knew that nobody was too small or too big to learn from.

"I don't ever want to stop learning and growing. It's not only valuable it's also *fun!*" he told me one time.

What a childlike wonder he has! It seems that is something we naturally lose when we become adults. We stop imagining and dreaming. We stop asking questions and being curious for fear of looking ignorant or foolish. What a shame! We shouldn't stop asking questions when we grow up. Our curiosity can unlock the door to continual creativity and wisdom. Our questions should simply get better.

> **"Our curiosity can unlock the door to continual creativity and wisdom."**

He also showed me something important that followed me for the rest of my life: *There is no organization or person too small that we cannot learn something from them, and there is no organization or person too big that they do not need to learn something.*

I have endeavored to keep that quality of childlike wonder—to be curious and ask those questions; to hunger constantly to learn more; to understand that there are lessons, both good and bad, in every situation; and there is always something from which I can learn and grow.

Leadership Lesson: No matter who or what the situation is, there is always something we can learn from it that will help us grow as human beings. Keep asking questions! Guard your childlike curiosity and wonder. It is one of our most valuable resources to maintain a fresh perspective as leaders.

APPLICATION:

- Do you cultivate your curiosity? How?

-

-

- Are you on a continual search for new and creative ideas?

-

-

-

- In meetings, do you ask more questions and listen more than you talk?

-

-

- Get a dream sheet (a blank sheet of paper) and write out some of your abandoned dreams. Keep your childlike wonder alive!

-

-

PART III

REV. FRED J. WARD

Fred J. Ward grew up in West Tennessee and became a leader in industries in Jackson, Tennessee. He worked for Conalco, ITT, and Bendix, to name a few. He was a plant manager and understood industry and business, but later in life, he felt a call to preach. He left an extremely lucrative job (he was married with small children at the time) and the next day became a freshman in college, making next to nothing and living on pure faith. He completed his degree in four years and began preaching at churches in the area.

He not only led national and international mission trips, but the churches he served were consistently leaders in growth and models for others to follow. In a county seat town, with about six thousand people, over six hundred people attended his church. That's a pretty significant community impact.

Fred had a strong streak of common sense that was combined with an ability to communicate it in a way that was unforgettable. I met Fred as a twenty-year-old student at a college, directing music part-time at his church, First Baptist Church of Huntingdon, Tennessee, and eventually moved into a full-time status. I served that church for almost four years.

I started as a boy, but I left as a man. Fred spent hours pouring his wisdom and knowledge into me. He viciously attacked my boneheaded mistakes and strongly reinforced me as a person. This was how he operated. He knew that leadership did not involve making followers. Leadership meant making other potential leaders ready to go out and do the same thing.

Fred passed away in June 2016, leaving a legacy of changed lives. I am blessed to be one of them. Here is the wit and wisdom of my spiritual father, my mentor, my pastor, and my friend.

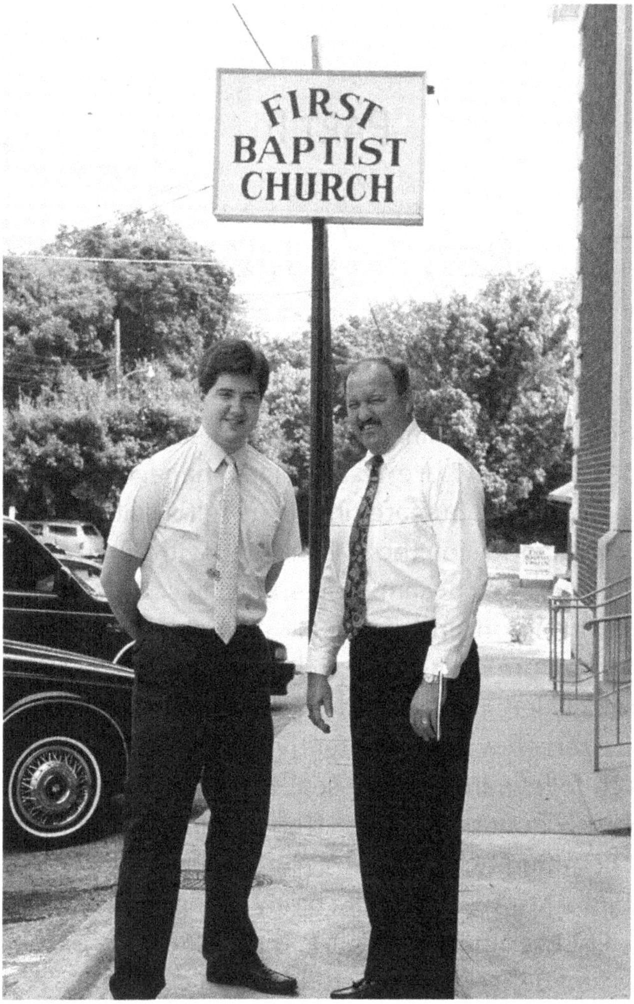
FIRST
BAPTIST
CHURCH

Chapter 14

Nothing Personal

If you're not a Baptist, you may not get this next part. Baptist churches have business meetings, and they can be very contentious. I had seen some tense moments growing up in a Baptist church, but nothing compared to my first business meeting when I was serving my first full-time church in Huntingdon, Tennessee.

The pastor of the church, Fred Ward, was trying to remodel the existing sanctuary and expand other places for additional classroom spaces. The growth of the church merited the space, and the poor condition of the auditorium (most recently updated about twenty years prior) called for the remodel. Money had been given toward this, and it was ready to roll.

Even so, a small contingency in the church (who had been members for many years) opposed Fred publicly. They said it was a dumb idea to spend money right now. There were some groans from people in the audience, and a couple stood up to oppose them. Words were exchanged in some loud tones. I honestly thought someone was eventually going to ask the other person to "step outside," but they didn't.

Eventually, a vote was called for and the measure passed. *Barely* passed. I'm talking by a razor-thin margin of two people. There were some boos and cheers afterward, and then the main spokesperson for the opposition group approached Fred and informed him that this wasn't over.

I followed Fred into his office and thought he would be upset, but he wasn't. He sat at his desk and said, "Well, that's over."

"Over! How could you just sit there and take that? I wanted to stand up and punch someone!" I replied incredulously.

Fred gave me a peculiar look and said, "Why, Ken? It wasn't personal. It was just business."

I sat there, staring in disbelief. He wasn't the least bit upset. The following week, I learned why he reacted that way.

We were in the middle of getting ready for a large Christmas presentation. If you don't know, Christmas musicals (especially in the early 1990s) were big deals at churches and involved lots of hours of preparation and work.

In the course of getting this ready, I was working long hours and late nights. One morning, a volunteer was critical of what I was doing, and I bit their head off. Keep in mind, they were a volunteer—coming on a weekday in the morning to help me, and I bit their head off. Even when I type that sentence today, I still cringe at my lack of awareness.

Fred heard it. He called me into his office. He absolutely chewed me up and spit me out.

"How could you say something so insensitive? Why are you out there doing everything yourself? Do you think you're too good to let other people help you? You need to get a governor on that mouth of yours before you start running people off! They're volunteering their time trying to help you, and you're chewing them out? Why would you punish someone for doing you a favor? That's the dumbest thing I've ever heard of! *Oh!* And you told me you were going to spend $350 for those lights, and they actually cost $600 by the time you got them shipped here. You need to budget better. If it was your own money, you'd be more careful. Quit being careless with the church's money!"

I was stunned. In tears, I thought, *I'm twenty years old and will never be successful at this. I'm a screwup. My boss hates me. How can I ever succeed when I'm this bad?*

What happened next not only shocked me more than what had been said, but it also forever changed my life.

Fred stood from behind his desk and calmly said, "Okay. Let's go get something to eat."

"Something to eat?" I thought the man was schizophrenic. "You hate my guts, and you want to eat with me?"

A tear was trickling down my face. Fred saw it and sat in the chair next to me. "What's wrong with you?"

After a moment, I said, "Why would you want to go eat with someone who is so bad?"

"So bad?" Fred asked in disbelief. "Listen to me, Ken. I never once said you were *bad*. I said what you *did* was wrong. You made some dumb mistakes out there, and I'm not going to let those go by without pointing them out. But it isn't because I think *you're* bad. It's because I see so much potential in you that I don't want to let you keep making those mistakes."

We went out to eat, and he continued talking to me.

"When I worked in industry for all those years, it was tough. If you messed up something, you expected to be dealt with, chewed out, cussed out, or even written up. That's just the way it was. [Fred never cussed at me, by the way.] But *they always attacked the problem; they never attacked the person*."

I asked, "Can you explain that a little more?"

"Yeah," he replied. "I said what you did was dumb. I didn't say *you* were dumb. In fact, if I actually thought you were dumb, I wouldn't have said anything. But I knew you were acting in a way that was not consistent with who you truly are. That's why I called it out. Do you understand that I can strongly disagree with you or dislike what you do and still love you as a person?"

I had never seen it that way.

Then Fred brought it all full circle and said, "See? It's nothing personal. It's just business."

I understood. At that point in my life, Fred Ward earned the right to tell me anything. As long as I knew he loved me, he could tell me anything he wanted because I knew it was always going to be in my best interest. The years at Huntingdon were some of my greatest years of personal growth because I had a mentor who loved me enough to tell me the truth about my shortcomings while encouraging me as a person to grow.

When I stepped into a leadership role, I tried to model what Fred had taught me—love people, attack problems. And if I don't truly love someone, I haven't earned the right to speak about their lives.

**"Love people. Attack problems.
If I don't truly love someone,
I haven't earned the right to speak about their lives."**

Fred once told me he was going to write a book about church life, and the name of the book was going to be *Nothing Personal*. He never did get to write that book. I think you'll agree that if he had expounded on this subject, it would have been a great one for every leader to read. We'll all just have to settle for my summary.

Leadership Lesson: Attack the problem but *never* attack a person. Make it about the problem or performance, but always reinforce the person. When you feel attacked, ask yourself, *Was that really a personal attack on me, or were they addressing what I did or said?*

APPLICATION:

- Have you been taking criticism personally?

-

- When you think back on the criticism, were they attacking you personally, or were they attacking the problem?

-

- Was it personal, or was it just business?

-

-

- Before you criticize anyone, ask yourself four important questions:

　1. Do I truly care about this person?

　2. Are my words meant to attack them or the problem?

　3. Is my intention to help them or wound them?

　4. How can I reinforce how I care for them and value them as a person before I speak about their issue?

Chapter 15

Stallions and Thoroughbreds

I'm an extremely driven person. So, when I do something, I go all out and do it. When I started in ministry, I was doing everything myself. I was working countless hours a week and loving every minute of it. There were several problems with this, though.

1. There was only so much I could do by myself.
2. I was robbing others of the blessing of getting to do what they could.
3. I was attempting to be some sort of valiant hero who slayed every problem that reared its ugly head.
4. I was robbing the important people in my life of my time.
5. I was burning out . . . *quickly*.

I was working at the church late one Wednesday night. Fred came through the auditorium and saw me feverishly doing things and commented, "Wow, Ken. You're quite a thoroughbred."

Whoa! I thought. *A thoroughbred! That's impressive!*

That is, until I learned the definition of a thoroughbred, which is "a fast horse that is good for short distances."

That is *not* what I wanted to be! I wanted to run a long race, but it was clear Fred was telling me I was on a short track to a quick finish. The next time I saw him, he had that knowing smile on his face, and I guess I did too.

"Thoroughbred, huh?" I asked with a smile.

"Yep," he replied. "You looked it up, didn't you?"

I nodded.

"I knew you would. I'm trying to help you."

I knew Fred's heart now and was confident he was teaching me something important. So, I inquired further, "I don't want to be a thoroughbred. But I don't know what I should be."

Fred responded, "You should be a stallion. A stallion is built for the long run. They can go fast for short distances when they need to, but they are also built for durability and enduring the long race. They don't just start well. They *finish well.*"

"A stallion is built for the long run."

Those words really resonated with me as Fred continued, "Some people will remember how you started, and a few will remember some of the things in the middle, but nearly everyone will remember how you finished. Finish well, Ken. Finish well." My father had told me something very similar when I resigned from a job to take another one.

Side note here: I know nothing about horses. There may be some horse trainers reading this and saying, "Well, that's not exactly true," and you're probably right. But for the application of this lesson, I didn't care. It truly resonated with me.

I thought of the old fable of the tortoise and the hare. The rabbit was fast, but the tortoise won the race because he finished well. As I'm writing this, I've been training for my first 5K. When you run, you don't focus on running fast. You slow down your pace and focus *first* on running for a certain amount of time. The distance eventually comes, but the goal isn't speed (at first); it's merely running without stopping. Once you master that, the speed can be added at the end, but it's not the focus. The focus is on running a 5K and *finishing*.

I understood what Fred was telling me. As he was leaving, he turned on his heel and added some final thoughts:

> One more thing, Ken. A stallion is also made to breed. In other words, they reproduce themselves. That's what true leaders do. Weak leaders generate followers, and when they move on, they leave a weak organization. Strong leaders reproduce themselves—as in other leaders. They pour into them, and

when they move on, they leave a strong and vibrant organization full of strong and vibrant leaders. Be a stallion, Ken, not a thoroughbred.

Leadership Lesson: A true leader is a stallion. They reproduce themselves. They reproduce other leaders, not followers. Also, they are not nearly as focused on running a fast race as they are on finishing the race well. Finish well!

APPLICATION:

- Are you working hard on the things and people that are priorities in your life?

-

-

- Who are you pouring into in order to reproduce yourself in your organization?

-

-

- Thinking about the end of your life, what would success look like for you? Be as specific as possible.

-

-

- What steps are you taking today to move in that direction?

-

-

Chapter 16

Hit Dogs

There had been some rumblings in the church about some new classes that had been started. To start those classes, people who had been in other classes for a while had to be pulled out to become teachers of the new classes. Several negative comments made their way back to Fred. They always seem to make their way back to the pastor in these settings.

The complaints reached him on Monday, but they were done anonymously, where the actual people complaining wouldn't identify themselves. They seemed content to complain behind the scenes. Sound familiar?

And so, on the next Wednesday night service, Fred chose to address the congregation about why we needed the new classes. He emphasized growth as the normal state of any healthy organism. He preached on the Great Commission and the mandate of Jesus to go make disciples. It was a masterpiece, and when he was done, there were many positive comments with a line of people telling him he had their support.

One man stood off on the side and didn't seem happy. He was pacing with a frown on his face.

Fred turned to him and called him by name. The man said, "I didn't appreciate what you just said."

"What are you talking about?"

The man continued, "Using the Bible like that to make me feel bad."

Fred gently replied, "I was simply preaching the word and explaining to everyone the direction I feel the Lord is leading us."

Gruffly, the man blurted back, "Well, I don't like it!" And then he stormed off, leaving me standing there behind Fred.

Fred turned back to me, and I said, "Wow. Why is he so mad?"

He smiled and replied, "If you throw a rock in a pack of dogs, the hit dog will holler every time."

Fred reminded me of a few weeks prior when I had spoken to the choir about being faithful in attending rehearsals and a man had gotten upset with me. I couldn't understand why. Fred then repeated, "The hit dog always hollers. You talked about faithfulness. He hasn't been faithful. You threw the rock. The hit dog hollered. You weren't intentionally throwing it at him. You were doing what you were supposed to do—setting the bar of leadership high—exactly where it should be."

I knew at that moment that the man who was complaining to Fred was also the man who was stirring up the trouble about the groups. He was the one who was complaining anonymously behind the scenes.

Then Fred added, "The truth will always be offensive to those who are hiding behind a lie. Speak it in love anyway."

Fred knew it was him all along, but he told me, "I actually understand where he's coming from. I'll call him tomorrow when he's calmed down."

I learned another lesson that day—it's important to view things from the perspective of the person who isn't like you and who doesn't agree with you. Try to understand their perspective before you impose your own. Fred showed that to me that day by his example.

> *"I'm not directing my preaching at anybody. I'm just shooting down in a barrel. I can't help it if you're down there." —Dr. Adrian Rogers*[3]

Leadership Lesson: Speak the truth to a group, and the hit dog will holler every time. A vision that is well laid out and given to your people will be bought into by many, but not by all. Lead on anyway.

APPLICATION:

- Are you doing an effective job of communicating your vision?

-

-

- What are some steps you can take to see that vision from somebody else's perspective besides your own?

-

-

- Does seeing that other perspective cause you to want to communicate it differently?

-

-

Chapter 17

Being a Genius

In my first three years of ministry, I made every possible mistake. I mean *dumb* mistakes. Careless. Lack of planning mistakes. Bad communication mistakes. Taking people for granted mistakes. "Walking over my volunteers" types of mistakes. Saying something I shouldn't have said mistakes.

When I started realizing the litany of bad decisions I was making, I started trying to avoid making mistakes. Actually, that isn't right. I stopped trying to do things that had the potential for me to make mistakes. I started playing it safe.

Fred, sensing my half-hearted effort, called me on it.

I explained that I was trying to avoid making more mistakes and making people mad. Fred smiled at this one and said, "Boy! If you don't want to make mistakes and don't want to make anybody mad, leadership isn't for you. You better get out now."

"If you would escape moral and physical assassination, do nothing, say nothing, be nothing—court obscurity, for only in oblivion does safety lie." – Elbert Hubbard[4]

This was another time where I sat there not knowing what to say.

Fred continued, "Always remember, the value isn't in the mistake. The value is in what you learn from the mistake. Take the lesson and don't make the same mistake again. You'll be just fine."

I got what he was saying. It's true. There is great value in our lives from our mistakes *if we learn from them.*

I now say it this way: A wise person learns from their mistakes. A genius learns from somebody else's.

> **"A wise person learns from their mistakes.
> A genius learns from somebody else's."**

I hope you're learning from my mistakes what *not* to do.

As Fred walked away from my office that day, he added, "The good news with you is that you do learn from your mistakes." And then he turned, looked back at me with a smile and a wink, and added, "And at the rate you're going, you'll be a genius in no time."

Leadership Lesson: Risks and mistakes are a part of the leadership journey. Realize that leadership is never a popularity contest. Learn from your mistakes. The power is in the lessons, not the mistakes. Take the lessons, let go of the mistakes, and don't repeat them.

APPLICATION:

List the last three mistakes you made:	List the lessons you learned from those mistakes:
Forget this	Never forget this. This is where the value is.

CHAPTER 18

BILL

Bill was a special-needs person who faithfully attended the church. He had no trouble speaking his mind, and what was in that mind made its way to his mouth very quickly. Bill sat in the second row, in the center of the church, right in front of the pulpit. At exactly 12:00 p.m., if Fred wasn't done preaching, Bill would grandly raise his arm in the air, bend his watch toward the front of his face, look up at Fred, and then point at his watch as if to say, "Time's up, Preacher!"

Occasionally, our men's ministry would have a prayer breakfast at 6:30 a.m. on a Saturday. As a young person who enjoyed sleeping, it wasn't my favorite thing to attend, but I did it anyway. The men who made breakfast often arrived at the church between 4:45 and 5:00 a.m. to make everything in time for the breakfast.

At one of the breakfast gatherings, Bill had piled a mountain of scrambled eggs onto his plate, and he had a spoon in one hand and fork in the other hand, shoveling the eggs into his mouth with both hands. Amused by it, one of the men who had worked so hard on the breakfast said, "Well, Bill . . . is it good?"

Bill stopped eating for a second, looked up at the man, and flatly replied, "I've had better." He then continued shoveling the eggs back into his mouth.

Another thing about Bill—he *loved* baseball. Baseball season was his thing.

One Sunday, Fred was preaching a message about heaven, and he wanted to end with the point, "The Father will see you all the way home." To conclude his message, he had a great story from his childhood about when he played baseball and got a hit that rolled to the fence. He heard the voice of his father yelling to him from the stands, "Keep going, Son! You got a hit! Run!"

Fred was pouring his heart into the story, but others were observing Bill, who was leaning forward, white knuckling the pew with eyes like saucers. He was into this story!

Fred continued, "I was rounding second base, and the outfielder hadn't even gotten to the ball, and I heard my father say, 'Come on home, boy! Come on home!' I was running as fast as I could to third!"

By this time, Bill's eyes were wide open, and he was halfway standing up. . . .

Fred said, "I got to third base, and my coach was signaling me to go home, but all I could hear was the voice of my father saying, 'Come on home, boy! Come on home! Come on home, boy! Come on home!'"

By this time, Bill was standing completely up. Keep in mind, he was sitting in the second row, in the center of the church, so everyone was noticing him now.

Fred said, "The cutoff man had the ball, but I was determined to make it home, like my father told me. The shortstop threw it home, and I slid and—"

Bill, at the top of his lungs, motioning like he was the umpire at the game, screamed, "Safe!"

The crowd erupted in laughter, and Bill, realizing it, eased back down into his seat.

Fred calmly said, "Yeah, Bill. I was safe. My father saw me home."

After the message, Fred laughed about it. Sure, it ruined the end of his message, but there was another message being preached at the same time.

Fred told me that when you serve others who can't serve themselves, it doesn't matter whether they get it or are grateful. You're not serving them; you're serving the Lord.

After all, isn't that what Jesus said? *"I tell you the truth, when you did it to one of the least of these my brothers and sisters, you were doing it to me!" (Matthew 25:40, NLT).*

Leadership Lesson: Help those who can't help themselves. It's the right thing to do.

APPLICATION:

- Go find the "least of these" and do something wonderful for them today, whether they appreciate it or not.

Chapter 19

Get Your Glove, Sidney

Fred coached Little League baseball when his boys were little. He coached with a guy named Gerald. One kid on the team, Sidney—how do I say this? Let's just say he wasn't the most aware and hardworking young person you've ever met.

Fred and Gerald made the team run laps around the field, which, to circle all the ball fields, was about half a mile. Sidney didn't like running laps. In fact, he showed up at one practice with an oversized (and obviously homemade) bandage wrapped around his ankle and said, "Sorry, Coach; I can't run today. I hurt my leg."

Gerald questioned him on it: "What did you do?"

Sidney stumbled around for a reason, and it was obvious he was lying. Gerald reached down and unwrapped the bandage, revealing a perfectly good leg and an embarrassed Sidney.

Gerald then said, "I tell you what, Sidney. Why don't you take ten laps around the field for me?"

Fred looked shocked and said, "Gerald?"

Gerald looked at Fred and said, "Oh, all right. Make it five."

Sidney looked up, smiled, and said gleefully, "Thanks, Gerald!" I guess he didn't realize how far he had to run to complete five laps until he reached lap three.

Fred relayed that story to me, and we laughed about it. Anytime Fred asked me to do something that seemed really difficult, I would always smile and say, "Thanks, Gerald!"

There was one time Fred asked me to do something that felt unreasonably hard to me, but Fred knew I was perfectly capable of doing it. I made a lame excuse as to why I couldn't do it. Truth be told, I was just being lazy.

Fred replied, "Okay then, you're fired."

"What?" I replied as my eyes went wide.

Fred said, "Sit down for a minute." (That was never a good thing if you haven't figured that out by now.)

"You remember Sidney?"

"Yes," I replied, still shaken up a bit. He then told me this story:

> Sidney never brought his glove to practice. He would always look at his teammates and me and say, "I ain't got no glove! I ain't got no glove!" We told him to get one, but he never did. Finally, the time came for Sydney, who was normally a benchwarmer, to go into the game. I told him to go check in with the umpire.
>
> He walked up to the umpire and said, "I ain't got no glove!"
>
> The umpire replied, "I don't care! Go tell your coach!"
>
> Sidney said, "I've been telling him!"

Then Fred looked me in the eye and said, "When the time came to go into the game, he made excuses. You can make progress, or you can make excuses, but you can't make both." And as he continued to look at me, he asked, "Now, are you gonna go get your glove and get in the game?"

> **"You can make progress, or you can make excuses, but you can't make both."**

I said, "Yes, sir. I will."

Fred said, "Okay, then you're hired again."

Leadership Lesson: Excuses are a dime a dozen. They're easy to find. We give ourselves permission to do things halfway all the time. Instead of using excuses, find the courage inside you, get your glove, and get in the game!

APPLICATION:

- Be honest! Have you been making excuses about why you couldn't do something, or have you been finding reasons why you *could* do it?

-

-

- Lay aside those excuses and make a list of five reasons why you *could* do something.

1.
2.
3.
4.
5.

- Now go do it!

-

-

Chapter 20

Drain the Swamp

Once, while working on a large event at the church, I was spending a ton of time (obsessively) working on one particular detail. Someone was in my ear telling me to do it. Fred pulled me aside and asked me why I was so hyper focused on something that in the end wouldn't matter. I told him about the other people who had been critical of what I was doing and how they were steering me toward working on this task.

He then asked a great question: "If they're so passionate about that one thing, why don't you let them do it so you can focus on what you're supposed to be doing?"

Per usual, he was right. Clearly, I had not thought of that.

Fred then said, "Look—your job is to drain the swamp. Right now, your pump is full of alligators. Get the alligators out of your pump and drain the swamp."

I had lost sight of the main goal while dealing with minutiae. It would be no different from a baseball player at the plate being obsessed with straightening his helmet while a strike flies by him. Straightening your helmet is okay, but it's definitely not more important than the pitch. A batter is at the plate to bat. A leader is in place to lead everyone toward the main thing, that is, the overall vision.

There are times as leaders that it becomes easy to major on minors and forget the overall vision. In doing so, you may win a battle, but you'll ultimately lose the war. That's never a good trade.

From that day on, whenever I was overseeing an event, I would always ask myself, *Am I still draining the swamp, or do I have some alligators in my pump clogging up the process?*

Leadership Lesson: As a leader, don't allow yourself to get so caught up in the small things that you lose sight of the overall mission and vision. You can empower and delegate others to take care of those things that keep you from seeing that the main thing remains the main thing.

APPLICATION:

- What are your *main* things?

-

-

- What is it that *only you* can do? Be honest with yourself. Delegate the rest.

-

-

- Are you majoring on the major things, or are you majoring on the minors? Majoring on minors can lead us to disaster.

-

-

CHAPTER 21

COUNT THE COST

It was January in Tennessee, and we had just completed an incredible Christmas season. We took our breaks, vacations, and were back at work for the new year. I had just started working full time at the church that week.

"What are you doing today?" Fred asked as he walked into my office.

"Oh . . . just working," I replied.

"On what?" he pressed further.

"I'm just cleaning off my desk and catching up on some things," I replied.

My reply told Fred what he wanted to know. He asked me, "Do you have a to-do list for today?"

I didn't. I'd never had a to-do list. Although I didn't immediately reply, the look on my face had already told him the answer.

"Let me ask you something else. Could I see your budget for the Christmas musical?"

"Sure," I answered as I found it under a pile of stuff and handed it to him. The budget was full of nice round figures.

Fred looked it over and then asked, "How much did you actually spend?" I'll just admit it. I had zero clue. I didn't really know. In the heat of the battle of getting things done, I had forgotten to stay accountable for the money.

Fred then showed me the budget bottom line and said, "I just did the numbers. You were $7,378 over budget."

My eyes got very large. I knew this was bad.

"The musical was phenomenal. The production was the best one this town has ever seen. Your musical direction was great." He paused before he continued. "Your administration stinks. You gotta get this stuff right or none of that other stuff matters."

With my twenty-two-year-old head down, I replied, "Yes, sir."

"Look at me. I'm not mad at you. Nobody's ever shown you this stuff, so I'm gonna show you how to do it right now. If you do it again, I will be mad. Doing this once is a mistake. Doing it twice is a choice."

He sat down and showed me how to budget and how to track it. He also taught me that when things aren't budgeted, I've probably planned poorly and haven't truly "counted the cost." He then quoted a Bible verse:

"For which of you, intending to build a tower, does not sit down first and count the cost, whether he has enough to finish it" (Luke 14:28, NKJV).

"You're the leader, Ken. You have to count the cost," he instructed. Then he continued, "And that doesn't just go for budgeting money. That goes for budgeting your time and even your life. You have to have a to-do list, or your day is going to control you. Failure to plan is planning to fail. You have to have a plan."

"This is difficult for me," I admitted.

"It will be at first, Ken," he replied, "but you *have* to do it."

Then Fred said one of the most profound things he ever said to me. I'm sure the quote didn't originate with him, but he was the first person to ever say it to me, and it immediately stuck. He said, "The hardest person you'll ever lead is yourself. You have to win the battle of self-discipline before you can lead other people effectively."

Fred then took me to his office and showed me his to-do list for the week. Then he flipped back in his notebook and had to-do lists for the previous weeks. He then helped me formulate mine. Now I was aware that I wasn't taking time out to sit and think through my week. I was just running headlong into each day, getting things done that crossed my path, and forgetting things that I had failed to plan for and write down. All of that ended that day with the creation of some much-needed lists. To this day, I keep to-do lists of what I need to accomplish daily, weekly, monthly, and annually in all areas of my life. I have markers set up to gauge my progress. It is a discipline I have learned, and it is now a habit.

People will occasionally ask me, "How do you get so much stuff done?" The answer is simple: I plan my work, and I work my plan. I count the cost with my money. I count the cost with my time. I count the cost with my priorities. I count the cost with my life.

A word of warning: If you don't have a plan for your life, somebody else does. Do you know what their plan is for your life? *Not much*. And that's exactly what they'll help you achieve.

Self-discipline isn't easy, but it is absolutely an essential quality every effective leader possesses, and the good news is, if you don't have it, you can acquire it.

Start with your to-do lists today.

> *"In reading the lives of great men, I found that the first victory they won was over themselves. Self-discipline with all of them came first."* —Harry S. Truman[5]

Leadership Lesson: Have a plan for your life in each area. Write out your goals, then break those goals down into monthly and weekly goals. Self-discipline is an acquired skill that takes an intentional plan and a lot of time, but it is ultimately the key to unlocking the life you've always wanted.

APPLICATION:

- Make a "to-do" list for the month.
-
-

- Make a "to-do" list for this week.
-
-

- Make a "to-do" list for today.
-
-

- Keep the daily list limited to three major points that align with your major mission in life. Keep those priorities (see the previous chapter)!

-

-

Chapter 22

The Leaf

It was September in Huntingdon, Tennessee. Football season was in full swing (which is a big deal in the South), and in the church, it was a season of turmoil. Between complaints and volatile business meetings (mentioned in an earlier chapter) exhaustion was setting in and affecting the staff.

After seven years at the church, Fred had had enough. He wanted to leave. Another church had called, and the circumstances seemed to dictate that this would be the perfect time to leave. I sat in the office with Fred discussing the situation. He wanted to get out of a bad situation, and the offer of another place was on the table. We discussed the exciting possibilities of a new opportunity, and then Fred did something...

In Bible terms, this is often referred to as "throwing down the fleece," which is a reference to Judges 6 when Gideon threw some fleece on the ground to get divine guidance.

Outside of Fred's office was a tree. The leaves were barely starting to change. One leaf stood out. It was oddly facing to the left at a 90-degree angle. It stood out conspicuously. Fred then said, "If that leaf falls off the tree in the next two weeks, I'm taking that as a sign that I need to leave."

One week went by, the leaves were turning all sorts of beautiful colors, and a few fell to the ground, but not "the" leaf. It stayed right where it had been, connected to the branch.

Two weeks later...still there. Three weeks...a lot of leaves had fallen, and that leaf remained. In fact, after *all* the leaves had fallen off that tree, that leaf remained connected. It withered a bit, but it *never* fell off the tree. Talk about a sign! Later that year, the entire tree was cut down to make room for a children's playground for the preschool. We joked that it took cutting the tree down for the leaf to fall!

Fred ended up staying at that church for over twenty years. He saw some of the best years of his ministry after the leaf that didn't fall. Several years later, Fred told me if he had left, it would've been a huge mistake and he would've missed out on so much. He said the Lord taught him an important lesson about evaluating things circumstantially.

Thank God for the leaf!

Living life means we will have good times and bad times. It's just a part of life. The Bible says it this way: *"(He) sends rain on the just and the unjust." (Matthew 5:45b, NKJV)*

Jim Rohn said it this way: "The same wind blows on us all. But it isn't the blowing of the wind, but rather the setting of the sail that determines our course."

"It isn't the blowing of the wind, but rather the setting of the sail that determines our course."– Jim Rohn

Fred looked at me all those years later and said, "Ken, don't ever leave someplace. Instead, go somewhere."

Simply put, don't run away from a situation just because it's difficult. Remember your reason for being there and your purpose. Press through the tough times, learn the important lessons, and then you'll actually be ready for your next assignment.

And you may just find that leaving your assignment too early may cause you to miss out on the some of the greatest successes of your life. Don't let adverse circumstances rob you of what could be some of your greatest successes. Perseverance can provide you with rewards that desertion never will.

Leadership Lesson: Tough times are assured. Tough people are not. Be the person who presses through to accomplish what you originally set out to do, then you'll be able to know whether it's right for you to move on or stay. Circumstances don't determine your direction in life. You do.

APPLICATIONS:

- Are you allowing adverse circumstances to determine your direction in life? What are some adjustments you could make to press through to the other side?

-

-

- If you pressed through, what rewards and life lessons could await you on the other side?

-

-

Chapter 23

Chameleons

Speaking of reading Fred's "to-do" lists, nobody could read them but him. It's not that his handwriting was illegible; it was his spelling. Fred spelled everything phonetically. In other words, in Fred's notes, "psychiatrist" would always start with an "S" and so did "tsunami." This made reading his notes next to impossible for anyone except Fred. He hand wrote out all of his messages, and that's the way he wanted it.

One day, I was in his office, and he was about to speak about standing up for your convictions. He then asked me about the name of the lizard that changes colors depending on its environment. I told him it was a "chameleon." He then asked me how to spell it, which I told him.

Come Sunday, Fred was preaching away:

"Oh, you change with the wind wherever you are. You don't stand up for what you believe. You stick your finger in the air and find out which way the wind is blowing and just go in that direction. You're like one of those . . . one of those …"

I could tell he was a bit confused as he looked down at his notes, and continued, "You're like one of those 'CHAM-A-LONS'!"

I died laughing; I guess I laughed because I knew the entire back story. His sweet wife, Lois, giggled too.

One Wednesday night after my music rehearsal, Fred could see that I was bothered by something, and he asked me what was wrong. I told him there was someone in the congregation asking me to sing a certain song and that as the music director my job wasn't to just sing what somebody wants to hear. After all, I told him, "I'm not a jukebox."

Fred said, "Let me ask you something, Ken. Is that a preference or is that a conviction?"

"Both," I replied.

"Are you sure?"

"I think so," I replied with a little less assurance than before. "It's hard to tell the difference sometimes."

"Not really," Fred said. "Here's how you tell: a preference is something you want, but if you don't get it, you can live without it. A conviction is something you can't live without. In fact, you'd die for it. When we get them confused, most of the time, we've allowed our own stubbornness to get into place, and we begin to substitute something that was a conviction with simply winning an argument to prove a point or to get our own way."

He continued teaching: "I'd die for the word of God. I'd die for Jesus. I'd die for my wife and children." Then, leaning in for effect, he said, "I wouldn't die for whether or not I was going to sing a song."

I smiled. "I'll sing that song this Sunday. I'm sorry for being stubborn."

Fred smiled back. "Don't lose your convictions. You need them. Stand up for them. Just recognize the difference between convictions and preferences. Everybody has preferences, and sometimes we have to compromise to preserve the greater good."

"Recognize the difference between convictions and preferences."

In organizations today, I see the source of quite a bit of conflict between people's preferences and their actual convictions. If it isn't worth dying for, then it generally isn't worth arguing about. The nature of a preference is that we're willing to meet in the middle with other people's preferences. It's called compromise, and it's part of getting along with others, including those we lead.

The nature of a conviction is something that cannot be compromised. We stand on them. We don't change with the environment. In other words, with preferences we can be chameleons, but with convictions we're leopards, and we don't change our spots or colors for anybody.

As leaders, we must know the difference between preferences and convictions.

Leadership Lesson: Know your convictions and stand by them. Those are hills worth dying on. Don't die on the hill of preference. Our preferences come from our personality traits. Convictions are based on universal truths.

APPLICATION:

- Make a list of your convictions. Remember that convictions represent the things you would die for.
-
-

Stand by all of these convictions but be willing to compromise and meet in the middle for your preferences.

Chapter 24

Charlie's Poop

If you haven't figured it out by now, there were quite a few "characters" living near Huntingdon. There were many days I felt like I was in an episode of *The Andy Griffith Show* in real life, so if you of think Mayberry characters, then you'll be pretty close to the truth. If Ernest T. Bass had a quiet neighbor in the woods, it probably would've been Charlie.

Charlie had lived in West Tennessee all his life. He wasn't quite "all there." He was very soft spoken, gentle, and nice when you talked to him. He came to church in a horse and buggy—and this was in the early 1990s. The buggy (and quite frankly the horse) looked like it came from the early 1900s. I don't think any of us actually knew how old he really was, and you couldn't necessarily tell by looking at him, but he was up there in age. He had his own quirks and own mannerisms, but all in all, he was generally a nice, quiet guy who didn't bug anybody else.

There was just this one thing—his personal hygiene left a lot to be desired. He had about six dogs that lived with him, and we were pretty sure they slept with him every night. He tried bringing his dogs into church a few times, but he was informed that wouldn't work and that he needed to leave them at home. So, when he came to church, he often smelled really bad.

But hey—we were okay with it. Most people were aware enough and sensitive enough not to say too much about it and accept him as he was. Sometimes, people would drop subtle hints by offering to allow him to use a shower at their house. Other hints were not so subtle: people gave him gifts like soap and shampoo. Unfortunately, Charlie never really caught on to any of them.

But there was this one Wednesday night when *it* happened.

Charlie showed up at church very early and sat in his normal pew (most everyone at a Baptist church has their pew), and we could smell him. Only this time, it wasn't the normal unpleasant smell. This was worse. Yeah—*that* kind of worse. We knew he'd had an "accident" in his pants, and now "pew" had a whole new meaning for us.

People weren't at the church yet. There was still time to do something about it. Fred had to deal with this. I couldn't imagine how he was going to confront this guy, but I had to hear it. I snuck into the auditorium on one side where I could hear what was going to happen.

Fred approached Charlie, and the conversation went something like this:

"Hey, Charlie."

"Howdy."

"Are you okay tonight?"

"Yup."

"Uh . . . Charlie . . . do you ever think about your hygiene?"

(Then there was a long pause as Fred realized Charlie didn't know what "hygiene" meant, figuratively and *literally*.)

Fred continued, "I mean, do you ever think about the way you smell?"

Charlie looked up at Fred and said, "Well, I tell you what. . . . I'm clean from hide to hair."

Fred very politely replied, "No, Charlie, actually you're not. In fact, I think you may have had an accident in your pants."

Then Charlie looked up at Fred again and asked, "Where do you live?"

Fred was taken aback by the question. "What do you mean?"

Charlie continued, "I've been a member of this church for thirty-five years!"

I could see a bit of red go up the back of Fred's neck as he replied, "I don't care how long you've been a member of this church. You ain't coming in here with poo-poo in your pants!"

He then told Charlie he'd have to leave and clean up before he came back. Charlie left that day and several of us had to clean up the mess left on the pews and disinfect the area.

The whole encounter was funny and sad all at the same time. Later that night, I asked Fred if he felt bad about how he had to talk to Charlie.

He told me, "It doesn't ever feel good to talk to someone like that, but it would be worse not to talk to them. That's not loving people."

I must've had a look on my face that told Fred I wasn't quite getting what he was saying.

Fred said, "Let me ask you something. If I see you walking around all day with your pants unzipped, then you get home and see that, knowing I've been around you all day, would you not wonder why I never told you? Would you maybe even be a little upset that I let you walk around in front of others that way?"

"Yeah, I probably would be upset," I replied.

"When we don't confront others over things that could hurt them because our own fear of what they'll think or our desire to be liked, we're loving ourselves more than we love them. That just isn't right. I confronted Charlie because I had to. I didn't enjoy anything about that. But if I truly love him, I have to help him. Don't ever forget that, Ken."

Then he continued the lesson, "When you confront someone, be sure you're doing it from a motivation of love and a motivation of helping them more than you're helping yourself. If you're thinking more about yourself and your desires when you talk to them, chances are good that your motivation is wrong. And when you do confront them, be as clear as you can be. Being clear is not being cruel. In fact, it's the opposite. *It's cruel to be unclear.* Most of the time, we avoid being clear and direct because we're more concerned about someone liking us than we are with truly helping them. Confrontation is like a shot from a doctor. It can sting for a second, but if the goal is to help the patient, you've done them a service and eventually they'll see it."

"It's cruel to be unclear."

Then Fred looked at me and said, "By the way, your pants are unzipped."

Immediately embarrassed, I turned around and looked down. They weren't unzipped.

He laughed and said, "Made you look."

> *Proverbs 27:6 (NKJV) says, "Faithful are the wounds of a friend."*
> *Ephesians 4:15 (NKJV) says, "But, speaking the truth in love . . ."*

Leadership Lesson: It is unkind to be unclear. Telling someone the truth to make them better is one of the most loving things we can ever do.

APPLICATION:

- In the space below, list some ways that you can speak the truth *in love* to someone who needs it.

-

-

Part IV

Dr. Ron Phillips Sr.

Ron Phillips has pastored for over fifty years. For over thirty of those years, he was the senior pastor at Central Baptist Church in Hixson (Chattanooga), Tennessee, later known as Abba's House. *Abba* is the Hebrew name for "Father." Ron has the heart of a father. Despite being older, I would watch him go from place to place, speaking to large crowds, and afterward, the number one demographic who approached him for pictures and to talk with him were inevitably youth, aged eighteen and under. They were naturally drawn to his fatherly heart. So many of them had bad relationships with their own fathers, and Pastor Ron brought a measure of healing to their hearts. It was always a beautiful thing to watch.

But it wasn't just young people he helped. He also did the same thing with his staff. I was privileged to serve as his music pastor for sixteen years. During those years, I got to be alongside him for many events and trips around the country and internationally.

Here are a few lessons I learned from another incredible spiritual father, Dr. Ron Phillips Sr.

Chapter 25

Be Real

One of the greatest things about Ron Phillips is that love him or hate him, you 100 percent know him. There is not a fake bone in his body. He's real. His feelings and his thoughts are written all over his face. His feelings and thoughts don't stay in his head very long either. They will shortly be coming out of this mouth. He can't keep a secret to save his life.

Some people might consider this to be a weakness. I personally do not. I believe it to be a phenomenal strength and one of the key reasons so many young people are drawn to him. The world we live in today is full of people who smile to your face and stab you once your back is turned. The world is full of people who say one thing and do another. I don't know if I've seen a generation who sniffs out hypocrisy and falsehood any quicker than the younger generation coming up.

Pastor Ron knew exactly who he was, and he wasn't going to change that for anybody. Ron was an imperfect person, like all of us, but he never tried to hide anything or pretend he was something he wasn't. He is simply himself, and it is beautiful to watch.

He endured intense criticism (more on this in the next chapter) from those who never had the courage to live this way, but he never let it deter him, even though it hurt him.

Anyone who is around Ron Phillips for any extended period of time will learn eight important things about him:

1. He loves God with all his heart.
2. He passionately loves his wife, who was and is his high school sweetheart.

3. He loves his kids and grandkids. They bring him great joy.
4. He loves the Bible. He has forgotten more about it than most people will ever know. He loves preaching the word and hearing the word preached.
5. He loves the church. He loves being around the church. He loves being around church people, especially other preachers.
6. He loves America and freedom.
7. He loves Israel and the people there.
8. He loves Alabama football.

I don't know these things about Brother Ron because he told me. I know these things about Brother Ron because he *showed* me. Every single minute of every single day I was around him, he lived out all of this not simply with his words, but with his actions.

When I think about Dr. Ron Phillips, I think back to my time in college when I was in the computer lab and saw the following poem on a screen. I printed it out, memorized it, and still quote it today:

I'd rather see a sermon than hear one any day.
I'd rather you walk beside me than merely point the way.
The eye is a more ready pupil than ever was the ear.
Good advice is often confusing, but example is always clear.[6]

One cannot change their actions if those actions don't represent who they truly are on the inside. The change will never be permanent until it is resident on the inside of you. True change must always occur on the inside before it will ever be *real* on the outside.

> **"Change will never be permanent until it is resident on the inside of you."**

One of the most wonderful things about Dr. Ron Phillips is he lives who he already *is*. Our actions are merely mirrors of our inner character.

Leadership Lesson: It is better to be disliked for who you are than to be liked for who you aren't. Be real. Be you. All the time. If the real you is not a reflection of who you want to be, you can change and become better.

APPLICATION:

- When you look on the inside, do you like who you see?

-

-

- Have you tried to change your actions without changing your identity?

-

-

- Think about what you want to do, then ask yourself, *Who do I have to become in order to do that?*

-

-

For example, instead of trying to stop smoking, think of this goal as changing your identity to live as a nonsmoker. That will help you change your actions more than a resolution.

Chapter 26

Timing

I traveled the world with Ron Phillips. I could characterize him as a nervous traveler, but I would say "impatient traveler" would be a better description. My job on those trips was to keep him away from the airport desk or hotel front desk. He would easily become impatient with people if they weren't right on top of things. And so, on trips, I would keep him away from there and serve what he needed. And when we traveled, he had to arrive *hours* before his flight. If they said arrive two hours prior to departure, he was there three hours prior.

Here's the truth about Pastor Ron: He values punctuality. Being punctual is being polite. Being late is rude, and it's unacceptable. And that's exactly how he sees it.

Early on, I was "punctually challenged." I remember one time with Fred Ward, when he spoke to me about being late. He handed me a cartoon of "BC," where a caveman hears a volcano rumbling in the distance. He stands up with resolve, then runs to a woman, grabs her, dips her, and plants a big kiss on her just as the volcano erupts behind them. The woman is completely wowed by the spectacular kiss, and the man says, "If you ain't got timing, you ain't got nothing!"

Once, at Central Baptist, I showed up three minutes late for a choir meeting that I had scheduled. I was talking to someone in the hallway about something that was critically important to them, and being late felt justified to me.

Brother Ron didn't feel that way. When he found out what had happened, he called me in and said, "You were late. You don't need to do that again."

I told him why. He shot back, "That's irrelevant."

I justified, "It was only three minutes."

He corrected me, "No, it wasn't. How many people were in the room?"

I said, "About two hundred."

"You were three minutes late with two hundred people in the room—that means you actually wasted six hundred minutes. Those people worked all day and volunteered to be here. When you don't show up on time, you've wasted their time. It's just rude and disrespectful. Don't do that again."

I meekly replied, "Yes, sir."

That lesson stuck with me.

As I was leaving that day, Pastor Ron told me, "Remember: on time is ten minutes early."

"On time is ten minutes early. – Dr. Ron Phillips"

I typed that out and have kept that saying in front of me on the back of my office door for ten years, and since that time Pastor Ron told me, I have endeavored to be there at least ten minutes early every single time. If I have been late for anything, it was either out of my control or an extreme circumstance.

> *"Better three hours early than a minute late."* —William Shakespeare

Leadership Lesson: Be on time. On time is ten minutes early. Don't waste the time of those you lead.

APPLICATION:

- Arrive ten minutes early for every appointment this week. Do whatever it takes.

-

-

- If you know you have an early morning meeting, go to bed earlier or wake up thirty minutes earlier.

-

-

- If you're chronically late (like I was!) consider changing your watch to ten minutes ahead.

-

-

- For some great time-management tips, I would highly recommend the late Stephen Covey's book *Seven Habits of Highly Effective People*. It helped me.

-

-

Chapter 27

Believe the Best

One of the most extraordinary things about Brother Ron is his ability to forget the bad and remember the good. There were times when someone had done something extremely bad to him, and he chose to forgive. And he not only forgave them, but he also truly forgot many of the bad things. He would give the benefit of the doubt to someone who, quite frankly, I found to be undeserving of it.

In other cases, people took advantage of his trusting and forgiving nature and even stole money from him. And yet—Ron loves them. Despite all of that! What a heart!

I talked to him one time about it, and he told me, "I just made a choice that I'm going to choose to believe the best about people, rather than assuming everyone is bad. Do you get used sometimes? Sure. But other times, people will surprise you. And sometimes, some people, even those with bad intentions, will rise to the level of your expectation. If I expect them to be bad, they will be. But if I believe the best, I've found that most people will rise to that expectation too."

My perspective shifted that day. I learned not to prejudge anyone but rather let their actions show me exactly who they are.

One time, I heard Dr. John Maxwell say at a conference that when he meets someone, in his mind, he slaps a big ten on their forehead, and he considers them to be that way until they prove him wrong.[7]

I like that. I think that's a much better way to live life. One way is negative, and the other is positive. Brother Ron chooses to look at people positively. I have learned to do the same thing.

Leadership Lesson: Believe the best about people, then let their actions justify that faith or prove otherwise.

APPLICATION:

- Choose to believe the best about people until they consistently prove you wrong.
-
-

Chapter 28

Forgive Others

Related to that last lesson, I watched people take advantage of Ron Phillips, but he would give them other chances. I'm talking grace beyond all measure. One time, I questioned him on it with a particular person, and he looked at me and said, "Well, Ken, hasn't Jesus forgiven you? Didn't He say if you don't forgive others, He won't forgive you?"

Ouch. The truth does sting.

Ron Phillips doesn't simply quote the Bible, he lives it. And part of that living means embracing grace and forgiveness. He modeled this in his everyday life for *years*. I wish I had a more profound story to tell you about him forgiving someone, but the problem is, I can't pinpoint just *one*. There are myriads of examples of him giving people second, third, fourth, and fifth chances. When others ran away and abandoned them for their mistakes, Brother Ron ran toward them.

"You can't hold on to things, Ken. Holding on to unforgiveness is like holding on to cancer in your body. It's not hurting anybody but you."

That image of cancer was near and dear to me, as you can imagine. I know Dad would've done did everything to eradicate that cancer from his body, but ultimately it got him. Why would I hold on to something in me that would destroy me from the inside out?

Once I embraced that picture, I've never held on to bitterness with anyone ever again. If something does come to my mind, I immediately make the choice to forgive at that moment.

Do I get used? Yes.

Do I get stepped on? Yes.

Do some people surprise me? Yes.

Am *I* walking in freedom? That's the important question by the way, and the answer is *yes*.

Leadership Lesson: Forgive others and live in freedom.

APPLICATION:

- As you read this, did someone you need to forgive pop into your thoughts? Forgive them today! Let it go. We'll talk about this more in a later chapter.

-

-

Chapter 29

Don't Quit!

I was done, had served the church for almost five years, and after looking ahead, I realized that I had no steam left in my engine. My vision was dried up. I had no energy. The ministry felt stagnant. I was depleted and desperate when I walked into Pastor Ron's office.

I told his secretary that I needed some time with him. I alerted her to tell him this was a bit of a crisis situation.

With my head down and my eyes averted, I told him, "I probably need to resign."

Puzzled, he asked, "What for?"

"I just don't have anything left in me to give. I don't feel like I have a vision and don't know what to do. There are probably hundreds of people who could step in and do this job for you better than what I'm doing. I don't want to be in the way, so I guess I just need to step aside so you can get that person."

Pastor Ron paused for a moment. It was probably only a few seconds, but it felt longer. He paused until I looked up at him, and then he said, "*That's* what this is about? Shut up and get out of here."

My raised eyebrows and sideways mouth now revealed that I was confused.

He asked me, "How long have you been here now? About five years?" I nodded yes. He continued, "You know what your problem is? You've never stayed anywhere longer than five years, and now you're out of your bag of tricks. Now you're going to actually have to dig in deep and find something you've never done before. You're going to have to ask God to help you find something new, instead of relying on what you've done everywhere else.

"You're going to have to decide what kind of leader you're going to be. There are a lot of migrant leaders who stay a few years, do their 'dog and pony' show, and then they pack up their bag of tricks and roll them out for a new place and repeat that process over and over.

"Or . . . you can be a shepherd like the Bible tells us to be and stay somewhere and get to know the people and grow up with them. There are blessings that only longevity can give you, Ken. That's going to be your choice. Now go back to your office and don't waste my time with this kind of junk."

A bit stunned, I got up and left. I went back down the hallway to my office and shut the door. As I sat down in my chair, I became aware that my mouth was still open, so I closed it. I sat there pondering what he'd said about migrant leaders.

Suddenly, the words of a previous mentor, Jim Whitmire, jumped back into my head. When I was a college student, he told me, "In five years, you're either living in the glory you've facilitated or the mess that you've made. Either way, it's on you."

Dr. Phillips was right. I never had the courage to stay anywhere and press through the tough times. About every four to five years, a leader has a choice to make in their organization. It's similar to the choice that a runner makes when they get to the threshold of about a mile. If they break through that seemingly tough barrier, they find they can continue on for miles. If they stop, then they're done. The same is true here.

So, I made a choice that day. I made a choice to stick with it. I made a choice to press through the tough times. I made a choice that I would get to know the people I was serving. I mean *really* get to know them.

My beginning years at this church weren't the smoothest. There was a contingency of people who were upset with me for not being my predecessor. Some of them actively worked against anything I did. There were others (the vast majority) who were extremely supportive. I made the choice to change some things to what I was more familiar with but did it the wrong way. In my haste to effect change, I moved too quickly and didn't get buy-in from the people. There are other mistakes, but you get the idea.

Here's what I found out: After I made the choice to stick it out, I was much more aware and sensitive to the needs of the people I was serving. I was—to be frank—as I should have been from the beginning. I also found out that when you own your mistakes and sincerely apologize to your people for them, most of them are willing to forgive you and even give you more respect for your transparency.

Pastor Ron taught me a huge lesson that day. Anybody with a modicum of talent and experience can migrate from place to place, do a little dance for a few years, then jump to another place and do the same thing. But they miss out on something huge if they do.

> R. U. Darby and his uncle found a gold mine in Colorado in the 1800s during the great gold rush. After bringing back equipment to drill, they found a much more limited supply and eventually gave up and sold their equipment to another man. That man took all their equipment back to the site with a mining engineer. The engineer realized that the Darby's had a poor understanding of fault lines and the gold was still there... just three feet away from where the Darbys had stopped. Quitting too soon cost them a fortune![8]

At the time of writing this book, I have completed twenty years at Abba's House (Central Baptist Church). My kids grew up here, met their spouses here, and my grandkids were born here. I've participated in baby dedications for parents who were in my preschool choirs at one time. I've received that call in the middle of the night, where a loved one was gravely ill, and the family wanted *me* there because I'd meant something to their family for years. I've even had some who have said, "You feel like a part of our family." Pastor Ron is right; there is a blessing in longevity. There are amazing things that happen if we just press through and stick to it.

> "Never give in, never give in, never, never, never, never-in nothing." —Winston Churchill[9]

Leadership Lessons from My Fathers | 125

Leadership Lesson: It's during those most difficult times that we, as leaders, must stay strong and press on. Longevity requires us to dig deeper than we have ever before, but it also offers its own unique set of rewards. Don't miss out on them!

APPLICATION:

- *Don't quit!*
-
-

Part V

Governor Mike Huckabee

Mike Huckabee was the governor of Arkansas from 1996 to 2007. Prior to that, he was a Southern Baptist pastor for many years. He is also a musician and a proficient bass player. That's actually how I met him. My youth choir from Georgia was on tour, and we stopped at a church in Arkansas where my friend pastored, and in walked the governor, who played the bass for my youth choir. I found him to be funny, engaging, and genuine. That was in 1998.

In 2016, I began traveling with Governor Huckabee to sing and perform illusion shows on his international tours of Israel, Italy, Greece, Turkey, and the Baltic countries, as well as Russia. It's been a privilege and an honor to be a part of his tours.

So even though I met him in 1998, I truly didn't get to know him until 2016. And now I can honestly say that after traveling the world with him and getting to know him, he is still just as funny, engaging, and genuine as the first day I met him. There is no pretense about him whatsoever. What you see on TV is exactly who he is 24/7. He wouldn't know how to be any other way, nor would I want him to be. He is a positive example to me in nearly every area of his life.

Here are a few of the ways he's taught me by the life he lives.

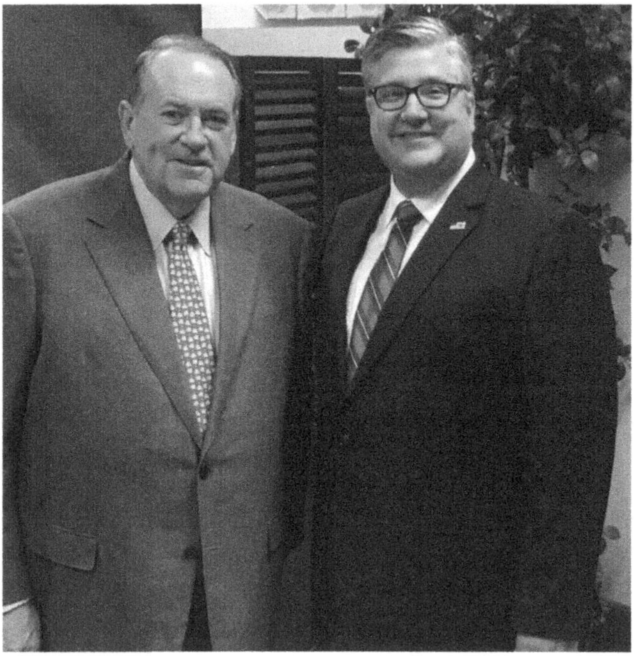

Chapter 30

Uncommon Ground

I grew up in Jackson, Tennessee. In middle school and high school, I was friends with Anthony. Anthony's father was my principal at Tigrett Junior High School. He was the principal you did *not* want to get into trouble with or mess around with in any way. Anthony was (to me) the principal's son, and we didn't know each other that well. In high school, Anthony and I had a civics class together. For those who don't know, civics is where they teach you the basics of how our government works.

The teacher in that class, Mrs. Hellen Mahaffy, always encouraged healthy debate on current issues. She was also the staff facilitator for an organization called Youth in Government. This organization gave us the opportunity to travel to our state capital in Nashville once a year, take the place of our representatives, and gain hands-on experience in how our legislative process works. I was the student president of that organization in Jackson.

To say that Anthony and I were polar opposites in our viewpoints would be an understatement. When debate time came, we would go at each other in class and vehemently disagree. I loved Ronald Reagan. He hated Ronald Reagan. You get the idea. And yet, after class, we would eat lunch together and laugh, and we enjoyed hanging out with each other. We didn't even consider doing otherwise.

Most of the participants in our Youth in Government organization believed the same things I did. I didn't think that was healthy. After all, what's the point of having a debate when everyone agrees with you?

One day in class, I looked at Anthony (after one of our classroom debates) and said, "You know, with a mouth like yours, you ought to be a lawyer or in politics." I invited him to Youth in Government, and he showed up. He represented a side that wasn't there.

It is likely that you've heard of Anthony. After Jackson, he went to school at the University of Tennessee at Martin and then to law school at Yale. He eventually became a special advisor for President Obama's Administration. Today, he is known as Van Jones. And yes, despite our political differences, *we're still very good friends today.*

Let's face it: politics is polarizing, and I don't recall a time that it has ever been as volatile and separated as it is today. Accusations and mudslinging abound. Social media and "keyboard cowboys" abound, and it has only poured gasoline on the fire.

While I was in Israel on one of my first trips, Van was celebrating a birthday. I sent him a video message, and Mike Huckabee overheard it. He said, "Are you talking to Van Jones?"

Uh-oh, I thought. *This might be bad...* But it wasn't.

Mike continued, "I love Van Jones! He is someone who, even though we don't agree, I respect. Can I send a video message with you?"

And we did. Van replied a few minutes later that it had made his day.

Mike and Van are political opposites, but they found common ground in other ways, or as Van would call it, *Uncommon Ground* (the title of his podcast).

Van had a show on CNN, and Mike had a show on Fox News and eventually TBN. Despite their differences, they have nonetheless supported each other as fellow believers. Long story short, this relationship ended up leading to a meaningful piece of bipartisan legislation (The First Step Act[10]) being passed and signed into law.

It is a rarity anymore to see people in our government meet on any middle ground. Compromising our preferences (see the previous chapter) is almost nonexistent. Most of what we see today is mudslinging, finger-pointing, an almost infantile set of accusations flying across aisles, and a complete gridlock because nobody can get along. Is it any wonder that the approval rating of the United States Congress remains less than 20 percent?

Mike and Van are friends who have learned to agree to disagree on some things, but they also know it is easy to find what we don't agree on. It's easy to point out how we're different. It's quite a different thing to find ways we are alike and choose to focus on them. You can have beliefs and convictions while still looking for common ground. That's what Mike and Van modeled.

> **"It's easy to point out how we're different. It's quite a different thing to find ways we are alike and chose to focus on them."**

Did Mike compromise his beliefs? No way. Did Van? Not an iota. They simply looked for common ground with each other and used that as a basis for an uncommon friendship.

Jimmy Stewart was a strong conservative. Henry Fonda was a committed liberal. Their political differences could not have been farther apart. The two actors almost got into a fistfight once over politics, and after a period of not speaking to each other, they decided their friendship was worth far more than their politics. When Henry's health was failing, Jimmy visited him two to three times a week. When Henry Fonda died, Jimmy Stewart simply stated, "I've just lost my best friend."[11]

Historically, this also happened with John Adams and Thomas Jefferson, with Herbert Hoover and Harry S. Truman, with Bill Clinton and George H. W. Bush., with Jesus and the tax collector, and with Jesus and the Samaritan woman.

There is great value in having a diversity of opinion. There is little value in conformity. Conformity exists where everyone not only has the same opinion but where they are also required to hold the same opinion. Diversity is like harmony. In music, three people singing the same part is called unison. It gets boring after a while. Harmony is three people singing different parts, but they all blend together to make something musically beautiful.

> *"If we both think and do and say the same thing all of the time, one of us is unnecessary."* —Dr. Delatorro McNeal, II[12]

I agree.

Leadership Lesson: Instead of looking for differences, look for similarities and start there. Leaders know that in order to get things done, we must set aside differences and work together for a greater cause and purpose. Leaders surround themselves with those who don't necessarily agree with their opinions because they know there is value in having a diversity of opinion.

APPLICATION:

- Have you surrounded yourself with diversity or with conformity?

-

-

- Determine to have a more diverse group of opinions that can lead you to possibilities you have not previously considered.

-

-

- Think of someone you don't get along with right now. Is there any common ground you can think of where you both can meet?

-

-

CHAPTER 31

THE GREATEST AMONG YOU

Let's face it. Governor Huckabee is a celebrity. He's a former governor and a former candidate for president of the United States. He has his own television show and is a frequent expert correspondent on the news. His daughter, Sarah, is a high-profile person, having served in President Trump's administration and now the first female governor of Arkansas. When we travel together, there is rarely a day I'm around him when someone doesn't ask for a picture or an autograph. I've also been occasionally shocked, when I've been near him, to see other famous people just walk up and introduce themselves to him. And yet—he's just a regular guy. He would say that himself, but his actions also show it every day. There is no pretense. There is no asking for special treatment or favors. In fact, it's quite the opposite.

The first trip I took with him to Israel was a small trip. There were only about forty people on the trip. To put that into perspective, when I go with him to Israel today, there are anywhere from two hundred to three hundred people on those trips on seven to eight different buses. On that first trip, though, we were all on one bus.

When people would encourage him to go first into a restaurant or a venue, he would graciously step aside and insist that they go first.

"Let nothing be done through selfish ambition or conceit, but in lowliness of mind let each esteem others better than himself" (Philippians 2:3, NKJV).

At one point in the trip, he bought some chocolate candy bars for everyone on the bus. For most people, it would've been enough for them to simply buy the bars and pass them back, but not Mike.

I watched (in awe) as he took the box of candy bars and slowly walked up the aisle of the bus, handing one to every person, calling them *by name* and thanking them for coming on the trip. It was extraordinary. Or was it? I found out he did the same thing on our big trips as well!

Why does he do this? Mike is simply showing the DNA of the Person he follows the most: Jesus. It is also the DNA of the greatest leaders throughout history.

"Yet it shall not be so among you; but whoever desires to be great among you, let him be your servant." (Matthew 20:26, NKJV).

The greatest leaders are those who serve the needs of those they lead. In speaking to people who have also known him for years and years, this is a consistent thread that runs through his life: serving the needs of those he leads. I've watched Mike model this over and over, and it has greatly influenced me in a positive way.

> **"The greatest leaders are those who serve the needs of those they lead."**

We are living in a society where many so-called leaders use their position and power to advance their own personal agenda in the way of monetary or personal gain. This type of behavior has fostered an atmosphere of suspicion and a lack of trust in leadership in general. Politics used to be known as "public service," but I doubt many in our society would see it that way today.

The only way to overcome this mistrust is through serving the needs of those we lead. It's not about us, our title, our position (which isn't leadership at all), or our gain; rather, it's about the people we're influencing and adding value to every day. That is the DNA of a leader.

Leadership Lesson: Leadership has little to do with you and everything to do with those you are leading. Serve the needs of those you lead.

APPLICATION:

- Below, list some specific ways you can serve the people you're influencing and leading.

-

-

CHAPTER 32

FIND THE LONERS

While on a trip to Israel, I noticed an elderly woman on our trip who seemed sad. After speaking with her for a minute, I found out that she and her husband had saved up for this trip to Israel for years, and a couple of months before the trip, he had passed away. Amazingly, she determined she was going to go on the trip anyway, because it's what he would have wanted.

Her loneliness was palpable and heartbreaking at the same time.

One of the places we visit in Israel was Masada. For the Americans reading this, think of Masada as the Valley Forge of Israel. It is a patriotic place for the Israeli people. It's set atop a large mesa—and quite a hike—and it's also one of the places I love to hear Governor Huckabee speak because it is a combination of theology, history, and patriotism.

On this occasion, I decided to ride to the top, but before we took the cable car up, I noticed that the elderly widow was sitting on a bench, and she told us, because of the walking required at the top, she felt like it was best to remain in the air-conditioned lobby and wait.

We ascended to the top where I sang, and Mike did his speech. I then noticed that he left the group pretty quickly, which was uncharacteristic of him. He normally hangs out, talks to people, walks along the tour, and interacts the entire time.

About ninety minutes later, I completed the tour (which is spectacular, by the way). When I descended in the cable car to the lobby, Mike was sitting next to the widow, just listening as she poured out her heart about the love of her life, their decades of marriage, how much she missed him, and how grateful she was to be on this trip that her late husband had bought for her—because he knew it was her dream to visit Israel.

The leader of this trip, the "celebrity," the one everyone wanted to talk with, sat quietly with the person who was the loner, and let her talk. There was no contrivance to this. Mike truly cared about what was happening in this person's life. I've seen him do things like this repeatedly.

Why? Because he cares. He really cares about people and what they're going through.

There were a few people who approached Mike for a photo as he was talking to the widow. He politely declined and kept his focus on her. At the end of the time, I watched as he and his wife prayed with her.

I learned a lesson that day. Not only did I see a beautiful example of leadership, but I became cognizant that Mike had no clue (nor cared) that I was watching him. He wasn't simply talking about leadership; he was *modeling* it. Leading by example is a much more valuable way of mentoring than simply telling someone what they should do.

> **"He wasn't simply talking about leadership; he was modeling it."**

Leadership Lessons: A leader truly cares for the people they're leading. If they don't care, they're not qualified to lead them. **Leadership is modeled.** *Be* the leader you're supposed to be. People are watching what you do more than they're listening to what you're saying.

APPLICATION:

- Write out some ways you can show the people you lead that you truly care about them.

-

-

- What are some specific steps you can take today to be a better leader?

-

-

Part VI

Bad Fathers

CHAPTER 33

BAD FATHERS

A quick word about this section. As I mentioned in the Introduction, I am a person of faith, and this chapter contains some more elements of that faith. If you find that offensive, feel free to skip it, but I hope you'll at least give it some consideration because the truths still work and are just as applicable today.

I know some of you who have been reading this don't have good relationships with your fathers. I get it. Although I had a wonderful relationship with my earthly father and many spiritual fathers, I have experienced dysfunctional relationships with authority figures who chose to be bad fathers.

In my time *in ministry,* among other things, I've faced challenging situations:

- I was physically threatened with harm.
- I was told I lacked ability and should just quit.
- I was offered money in exchange for providing people for baptisms to bolster end-of-the-year reporting numbers.
- A "leader" threatened me in the past and said they were going to lie and tell anybody anything they had to say to ruin me.
- A leader once lied about me to cover up something he did. (It was later exposed, and the truth came out.)
- I was encouraged to lie to cover up things.
- My kids were insulted, hurt, threatened, and verbally abused.

These are a few of things I've experienced in my thirty-five years of service in ministry. I have friends who have experienced much worse.

Let me be clear here: I am *not* down on the church. I love the local church, believe the church is the greatest hope for the world, and will be connected to a local church for as long as I live on this earth. The vast majority of leaders I've served with in ministry have been people of integrity who love God and love people, and I've had at least twenty good experiences for every bad one I've encountered that I've listed above. My point is, however, there are bad leaders in churches, just as there are in the corporate world. It's sad, but true.

People expect perfection from their church leaders and its members, not realizing that they are fallible, hurting people, just like everyone else. They are simply seeking help within the church, and I applaud them for doing so. The point is: people are people everywhere.

So why are there bad fathers? I believe it's because many leaders are too busy building their own kingdom. No matter whether the organization is secular or faith based, people flock to a mission more than they rally to someone's personal empire.

So how do you recover from things like this when you've been deeply hurt by someone who was either a bad earthly father or a bad father figure?

1. Forgive. This is step one. We touched on this in an earlier chapter, but let's expound upon it now.

Let's be clear about what forgiveness is and is not.
Forgiveness is *not* saying, "What you did was okay."
Forgiveness is *not* saying, "I excuse what was done to me."
Forgiveness is *not* saying, "I invite you to do what you did again."
Forgiveness is *not* saying, "I want to hang out with you again and talk all the time."
Forgiveness is *not* saying, "Everything is going to be exactly like it was before." It may be. Sometimes, it may be better. But it may not be either.

Forgiveness *is* choosing not to hold on to what was done to you.

Forgiveness *is* choosing to let it go.

Forgiveness *is* the realization that holding on to unforgiveness and bitterness is only hurting you (like the cancer Ron Phillips mentioned to me).

Forgiveness *is* the realization that as long as you hold on to unforgiveness, you'll always be chained to that person—and very likely they haven't given you a second thought.

Forgiveness *is* a decision we make with our minds and spirits that will emotionally work its way out for a long period of time.

My favorite quote on forgiveness is, "To forgive someone is to set a prisoner free and discover that the prisoner was you."- Lewis B. Smedes[13]

"To forgive someone is to set a prisoner free and discover that the prisoner was you." – Lewis B. Smedes

For some people, forgiveness isn't a matter of trauma but a simple disagreement that got out of hand and compounded through the years into a huge gulf between you. I would encourage you to have a conversation with them to resolve the issue. Put aside the feelings, and focus on the restoration of the relationship.

In the '80s, Mike Rutherford of Mike and the Mechanics cowrote a powerful song about his father that speaks to this:

> *Say it loud*
> *Say it clear*
> *You can listen as well as you hear*
> *It's too late when we die*
> *to admit we don't see eye to eye*[14]

You may never see eye to eye on everything, and that's okay. But you can choose to walk together despite the differences.

Through the years, I have encouraged people to let things go—even traumatic experiences. Do you have to do it directly to the person? I'll be honest; it helps, but it isn't absolutely necessary, and many times, they likely have no clue they've hurt you. I've even encouraged people to write a letter they will never send or even visit a graveyard for someone who is deceased. You'll be surprised how freeing this will be for you if you follow through and actually do it.

I also realize that for some people, making the choice to forgive seems next to impossible. The wounds are severe and deep. Do it anyway. Your freedom is waiting for you just on the other side of it.

2. Understand that every person, regardless of their position or title, is a fallible human being.

People let us down. They always have, and they always will.

One of the reasons I struggled in this area was false expectations. My dad addressed this with me (in an earlier chapter).

As you know, the first full-time pastor I ever served with was Fred Ward. He was a shining example of what a spiritual father should be, had integrity, and never shaded the truth. Not once. He said what he meant and meant what he said. He encouraged the best in you and others and modeled true leadership. In my youth and naivety, I just thought every pastor was going to be just like him. I really had no clue.

Truth be told, it was good *and bad* to have Fred as my first pastor because he set the bar so high. But part of the problem wasn't with the leaders I served with afterward. The problem was with *me*. That's right. Me.

I had expectations that each of them would be like Fred, and nobody was Fred except, of course, Fred. It was an unfair expectation. Expectations often lead us to disappointment and hurt. I should have taken the time to get to know each person better.

Don't get me wrong. I served with some great pastors. Bob Eliott, Fred Ward, Frank Cox, Ron Phillips, and my current pastor, Ronnie Phillips Jr., are all quality people who truly love the Lord and love people. But they're not perfect. Neither am I. Neither are you.

When we expect perfection from anybody other than Jesus, we'll always be disappointed, which brings me to the next point.

3. Keep your eyes on God, not men.

I am a person of faith. It may not be your faith, and that's okay. If it isn't, I hope you'll explore it and see for yourself. God has never disappointed me. Man has. I keep my eyes on Him. The closer I get to Him, the less the opinions of others matter to me. The more focused I am on pleasing Him, the less concerned I am with others' negative comments or experiences.

4. If you had a bad example in the past, make the commitment to be a good example now.

Find someone you respect in leadership and let them mentor you. Let their positive example be poured into you. Whether it's mentorship in person or mentorship via books and audios, it can help just the same. You can learn from the mistakes of those who did you wrong and choose to let that legacy of bad leadership die with them.

Recovery is a journey. In extreme cases, I would also recommend a good therapist to help you sort out your trauma in healthy ways.

The Hebrew word for Daddy is *Abba*. Several years ago, I was in the airport in Tel Aviv, Israel, where a young boy had lost his father. He was crying out, "Abba! Abba!" His father quickly found him, but that instance served as a reminder to me. For those who have had poor relationships (or no relationship) with their father, we have an Abba Father who is simply waiting for us to call out to Him. In fact, He is waiting right now for you to call out His name. Call on Him today. He's never let me down and has led me positively, and I believe He'll do the same thing for you.

Just like there are bad fathers, there are also bad sons. There are moments when you, as a leader, pour yourself into someone, only to have them ignore what you said and perhaps do the exact opposite. Some people will choose to betray you, and it hurts.

There have been seasons in my life when I was the bad son. I deeply regret them today.

In this instance, the easiest thing to do is to write off a bad son, but I would encourage you to do something a little different.

There is a story in the Bible about a son who took his entire inheritance from his father and went away and wasted all the money on wild living. He spent all the money doing everything his wild heart desired, and when the money was gone, he was left in a hopeless state. When I say hopeless, I mean he was living in a pigpen, eating whatever the pigs discarded.

After that, the story states that he "came to himself" and realized that the workers in his father's house lived better than he was living, so he decided to go back to his house and beg his father to let him simply be a worker, knowing he had forfeited the right to be a son.

But that's not what happened.

Jesus (the One telling this story) said the father saw the wayward (or prodigal) son afar off and ran to him and kissed him. He put his own robe on his son.

The point is this: there was never a time—not one time—that he wasn't still that father's son. Even when he was living in a way that was the opposite of what the father wanted for him. The father kept looking for him to come home, and when he did, he welcomed him with open arms and a party.

There are seasons when a son, biological or spiritual, may take the way of the prodigal. As a father, I would encourage you not to give up on them. And when they come back, don't punish them. Instead, give them a party.

And if you're a son who knows you've gone the way of the prodigal, I would encourage you today—your Father is just waiting on you to come home to Him. No matter what you've done, He'll greet you with forgiveness and open arms if you just ask Him.

APPLICATION:

- If you've never asked your Heavenly Father to forgive your sin, He is just a prayer away.

-

-

- You come to the Father through His Son, Jesus (John 14:6).

-

-

- Ask Jesus to forgive your sin and to be your Savior today. You and your Heavenly Father will have the most loving relationship that you could ever have with anybody on this earth. There will be a party in heaven when you do (Luke 15:10)!

-

-

Conclusion

June 17, 2000

7:20 p.m.

While the steady stream of visitors was being fielded outside of Dad's hospital room, I was in the room with him. The pain was becoming unbearable, and the doctors had prescribed some more potent medications to help ease the pain and help him rest. There are some people who would say that patients hallucinate, but I don't believe that's what happened in his case.

Here's exactly what happened next.

Dad called for me: "Kenny?"
I said, "Yes, sir. I'm here. Do you need anything?"
He paused for a moment, then replied, "Can you help me cover up?"
I pulled the covers up to his neck and started to tuck them around him, but when I did, he reached around and hugged me. Dad came from a generation where you didn't show a lot of emotion or affection, so this was monumental to me.
He said, "I'm so proud of you, Son."
I hugged him back and said, "I love you, Dad."
He said, "I love you, too, Son. I've always loved you with all my heart."
The flood of tears began pouring down my face as I tucked the covers around him.

After a few minutes of silence, I heard him say, "I tried. I tried."
"Tried what, Dad?" I asked.

"I tried to be a good son."

I had watched my father make the sixteen-hour round trips to my grandmother's house in Joplin, Missouri, to take care of her over and over. While he was there, he took care of everything for her. When her health really began to slip, those trips became more frequent. He was an incredible example of what a good son should be.

So, I replied, "You were a good son. You were the best."

He lay there for a moment with his eyes closed, then said, "Thank you. Thank you, Dad. I tried. It's so good to see you again."

In the Bible, Acts 7:55 states that Stephen looked into heaven and saw Jesus. Say what you want, but at that time, I believe my dad was looking into heaven and was more over there than he was over here. I think he saw his mom and dad, who had both gone to heaven.

He didn't say anything for the next fifteen minutes or so. Then he said, "Son, are you there?"

I replied, "Yes, sir."

"Get my coat."

"Are you going somewhere?"

He replied, "It looks like it."

"Where?" I asked.

He paused, then said, "The Lord is my shepherd."

I paused for a second, somewhat taken aback, and then I said, "I shall not want."

He said, "He maketh me to lie down in green pastures."

"He leadeth me beside still waters."

"He restoreth my soul."

"He leads me in the paths of righteousness for his name's sake."

Then, in a voice that was louder and stronger than I had heard him speak in weeks, he said, "Yea, though I walk through the valley of the shadow of death, I will fear no evil: for Thou art with me!"

Through my tears, I continued, "Thy rod and Thy staff they comfort me."

"Thou preparest a table before me in the presence of mine enemies."

"Thou anointest my head with oil; my cup runneth over."

Then dad finished, "Surely goodness and mercy shall follow me all the days of my life: and I will dwell in the house of the Lord for ever."

I mouthed, "Amen."

We completed Psalm 23 (KJV) in its entirety together. It was a moment I'll never forget.

Dad didn't talk for a while after that. I couldn't talk. I sat there in silence, praying through my tears.

Then he said, "It's been a wonderful life."

After a brief pause, he said with wonder, "Wow!"

Curious, I asked, "What do you see, Dad?"

He said, "It looks like we're going to sit down and have something to eat." I thought about the verse he had just quoted about God preparing a table before us.

I said, "Do me a favor."

He replied, "Sure, Son. What is it?"

"Save me a seat."

He said, "I'll do it."

And those were the last words we spoke on this earth.

Psalm 116:15 (NKJV) says, *"Precious in the sight of the Lord is the death of His saints."* On June 17, 2000, that verse became real to me. As much as was humanly possible, I watched my father go to heaven. I know someday I'll see him again.

I love that he died with no regrets: *"It's been a wonderful life."*

I pray the same is true for me and my kids.

But before I go, I know my mandate. My mandate is to be a good earthly father to my children, and I'm dedicated to serving as a good spiritual father to those in need of it.

If your relationship with your father is not a good one, make the commitment today to have healthy relationships with your family and those you influence. If your relationship is good, then pass on what you have learned.

The most valuable thing we can pass on is not our money or material possessions. The most valuable thing we can pass on to our kids (biological or otherwise) is our wisdom, love, knowledge, and godliness. Those are the things that last. Those are the things that make life worthwhile.

That is the essence of legacy. Legacy is that which lives on after we're gone.

> *For though you might have ten thousand instructors in Christ, yet you do not have many fathers; for in Christ Jesus I have begotten you through the gospel. Therefore I urge you, imitate me. For this reason I have sent Timothy to you, who is my beloved and faithful son in the Lord, who will remind you of my ways in Christ, as I teach everywhere in every church. (I Corinthians 4:15–17, NKJV).*

Teachers tell us what to do and grade us on it. Fathers walk the journey with us and lead by example, not by theory. They love us with the truth. In writing to the church in Corinth, Paul was sending them his legacy in the form of Timothy. He had poured his truth, love, and knowledge into Timothy, and in doing so, he multiplied himself.

The essence of legacy is pouring yourself into others to multiply your influence in a positive way after you're gone.

> *"Leadership is influence, the ability of one person to influence others to follow his or her lead."* —J. Oswald Sanders[15]

I agree. Leadership is influence, but it's also morally neutral. That means our influence can be positive or negative. We all have a choice to allow our leadership to influence people in such a positive way that it will have a positive impact on them for the rest of their lives.

One common thread from my father, through Jim Whitmire, Fred Ward, Ron Phillips, and Mike Huckabee, is that they all, at one time or another, have told me the truth, in love. They didn't simply tell me what I wanted to hear. They told me what I *needed* to hear and had *earned* the right to do so by their character, integrity, and their love for me, which was demonstrated clearly in their words and actions.

In many ways, I am doing what I Corinthians 4:16 above says. I saw what they did and am imitating them. And in imitating them, I am a better leader. In imitating them, I am a better person. In imitating them, I am closer to the Lord and becoming more like Him.

We are not human doings. We are human *beings*. Our job today is to *be* the leader who positively influences others and inspires others to emulate our behavior.

I hope some of the leadership lessons from my earthly and spiritual fathers have resonated with you. I hope it provokes deeper thoughts about your own leadership journey and causes you to grow deeper and give more to others. I hope it has you thinking about lives of others that you can change through the gifts, knowledge, and wisdom inside you.

Be the leader you're called to be. This world needs you!

Be a father to your family. They need you.

Be a spiritual father to those who are hungry to do more and be more. They need you.

Be a son of God the Father. We *all* need Him!

> *"Focus on the important things. The other things will take care of themselves."* — Dr. Kenneth R. Hartley, Sr.

About Ken Hartley:

Ken Hartley is an international keynote speaker and has authored (some as a contributor and as a coauthor) ten books, including Hidden Treasures, Leadership Illusions, God-Wired, and the Amazon bestseller, DISCover Your Team's Potential. He has several certifications in speaking, leadership, and is a Human Behavioral Specialist in the DISC model of human behavior. He travels extensively speaking to corporations and organizations about leadership, personal growth, and effective communication. His presentations combine his skills as a speaker, an illusionist, and a singer and are often described as entertaining, engaging, and transformational. He and his family reside in Chattanooga, Tennessee.

For more of Ken's leadership and communication resources, go to www.hartleyleadership.com

To book Ken to speak at your next event, go to www.hartleyleadership.com/contact

For more information about Ken, go to www.kenhartley.com

ENDNOTES

1 Get Motivated Seminar, 2009, Spokane, Washington

2 https://quoteinvestigator.com/2016/01/12/persist/

3 Nationwide Bible Conference, Bellevue Baptist Church, July, 1993

4 Little Journeys to the Homes of American Statesmen, Elbert Hubbard, 1898

5 https://www.truman.edu/about/history/our-namesake/truman-quotes/

6 From a poem by Edgar Guest

7 International Maxwell Certification, Orlando, Florida, August 2018

8 https://jric.wordpress.com/2008/06/30/the-story-of-r-u-darby/

9 Winston Churchill at Harrow School, October 29, 1941

10 https://www.bop.gov/inmates/fsa/overview.jsp

11 From the "Friends to the End" exhibit at the James M. Stewart Museum in Indiana, Pennsylvania

12 FTX Conference, Tampa, Florida, July, 2019

13 Forgive and Forget: Healing the Hurts We Don't Deserve, Lewis B. Smedes, Harper, 1984

14 The Living Years, Mike and the Mechanics, 1988

15 Spiritual Leadership, Moody Publishers, Chicago, 1967